Child Influencers

For Carissa, forever my favourite child.

Child Influencers

How Children Become Entangled with Social Media Fame

CRYSTAL ABIDIN

polity

First published in 2026 by Polity Press Ltd.

Polity Press Ltd.
65 Bridge Street
Cambridge CB2 1UR, UK

Polity Press Ltd.
111 River Street
Hoboken, NJ 07030, USA

ISBN-13: 978-1-5095-6802-4
ISBN-13: 978-1-5095-6803-1 (pb)

A catalogue record for this book is available from the British Library.

Library of Congress Control Number: 2025937703

Typeset in 11 on 14pt Warnock Pro
by Cheshire Typesetting Ltd, Cuddington, Cheshire
Printed and bound in Great Britain by CPI Group (UK) Ltd, Croydon

For further information on Polity, visit our website:
politybooks.com

Contents

Preface

This book is a culmination of eleven pieces of writing that I have published on child Influencers and related phenomena between 2011 and 2023. In these works, I have offered some new concepts, theories, frameworks, and ways of thinking about children and internet fame, but they have not yet been consolidated in a coherent collection. The book connects the various stints of fieldwork I have conducted on how children become entangled with social media through longitudinal and cross-generational ethnographic fieldwork dating back to 2008; the first generation of 'teen bloggers' whom I had first interviewed then and followed through the years have now transited across their life course to become parenting Influencers, and the landscape of social media has evolved significantly. Collectively, the chapters look specifically at the emergence of different types of child internet celebrity, and children's entanglements with online fame more generally.

Why Write a Book on Children and Social Media Fame?

At the time of writing, there are now about twenty scholarly books on Influencer cultures and related concepts published since 2008. These have tended to focus on a specific country market, content genre or platform. A vast majority of these books have focused specifically on young women, and others that have included other genders do so by way of investigating a platform more specifically. Most of these books have also focused on YouTube and Instagram. At present, there has yet to be a book looking specifically at age as a focus.

In response, this book will be the first consolidated effort to map out the extensive varieties of how children become entangled with social media fame and commerce as pathways towards becoming Influencers; to locate the historical milestones of concerns, scandals and changing public discourse that have resulted in important pivots in the ways we perceive the presence of child Influencers; and most importantly, to offer scholarly provocations on the key ideas, concepts and frameworks that can help everyday readers understand the phenomenon of children and online fame, and why it has proliferated so quickly in society.

Why should I be writing this book? As the saying goes, I was at the right place at the right time – quite literally. I was born in the late 1980s on the tiny nation-island-city-state of Singapore. For the unacquainted (or those who only know the 'Crazy Rich Asians' version of Singapore), the brief implication is that I was born into a society during a time when consumption and consumerism was fast on the rise among citizens during an economic boom; where education and job status continue to be increasingly competitive; where information technology advances rapidly due to the government's extensive investment in education, infrastructure, talents and citizen policy; and where the incumbent political party generally has a stronghold over national broadsheets, such that internet culture is a flourishing space of creativity and subversion.

I was a child but lucid enough to remember and understand when pagers/beepers were first introduced in the country (Hello Kitty pagers were a very rare commodity and I eventually persuaded my parents to buy me one at age eleven after scoring straight As in my exams); when my parents purchased their first super massive and heavy brick-sized handphones (when they were decommissioned we used them as paperweights at home); when modems became affordable enough for households to each purchase their own (I was among the children to be constantly yelled at for using the phone when the modem was trying to connect); when boxed-sized desktops were replaced by flat screen desktops, then laptops, then a whole suite of mobile devices (I appreciate the gradual release of more tabletop space); and when wireless and Bluetooth technology was rolled out nationally, island-wide. I was also 'extremely online' by the time the first generation of bloggers in Singapore and the Southeast Asian region became active and prolific online, and followed the crowd across the myriad of new platforms to come (we miss you LiveJournal, we miss you Friendster).

More importantly, even as I had front-row seats to watch the emergence of bloggers becoming commercial bloggers, then eventually microcelebrities, Influencers, creators and the like, I saw them in person all the time. When I first started seriously studying Influencers as an undergraduate, Singapore's land size was 705 square kilometres and its population was 4.5 million. When I had commenced my PhD research and then my first postdoc, its population was 5.1 million and 5.6 million respectively. As I write this book in 2024, Singapore's population has burgeoned to over 6 million people, and through some land reclamation efforts its land size has increased slightly to 735 square kilometres. All this is to say: While I followed Influencers online, I also saw them in the flesh all the time. And as my longitudinal ethnographies on the Influencer industry became more honed with training and maturity, I had increasing access to the backend of the industry through my anthropological fieldwork.

I also wrote one of the first PhD theses on Influencers as a professional career and industry (Abidin 2016); one of the appendices details the emergence of the very first cohort of children born to the pioneering generation of Influencers in the country, and how grooming 'internet famous' children was a nascent trend. At the time of writing, 'internet famous' children are commonplace, mainstream, ten a penny. As such, this book is informed by close to two decades of anthropological study on the Influencer industry and the larger culture of internet celebrity, but focuses specifically on how children have become entangled with social media fame.

Every day, the buffet of risks for children who engage with digital cultures is multiplying, but so are the opportunities. At the time of writing, I work as Associate Investigator at the Australian Research Council (ARC) Centre of Excellence for the Digital Child, the 'world's first research centre dedicated to creating positive digital childhoods for all Australian children' that aims to shape 'a future where every child can thrive in the digital age' (Digital Child 2024). I have the privilege of working with world-class researchers who focus on fostering 'healthy digital lives', 'educational empowerment' and 'safe digital spaces' for young children (Digital Child 2024). I also recently completed a four-year Asia Pacific-wide project to study how social media Influencers act as conduits of knowledge, funded by the Australian government's ARC Discovery Early Career Researcher Award (DE190100789). These two portfolios explain the book's specific interest in the digital lives of 'internet famous' children, with several case studies throughout the book drawn from across the Asia Pacific region.

Parting Words

I might be misperceived as being an enthusiastic proponent of turning your child 'internet famous', because this book is not constantly overtly critical of the phenomenon. It certainly does raise, across several chapters, the very pressing concerns in the industry and criticisms of some of the existing practices. But the case studies also point to moments of hope and play, instances of carefully calculated decisions when guardians balance online visibility with its perks, and room for the industry to improve and professionalize. The reality is that child Influencers are likely to remain in our society for a long time, for as long as digital platforms and cultures continue to be all-pervasive in our lives, for as long as late-stage capitalism is pushing individuals to seek creative employment and income streams amidst widespread precarity, for as long as the cuteness and chaos of children continue to attract our attention. And so the solution (for me, at least) is to conduct more research, provide more contextualized nuance and produce more situated frameworks, to better inform the grassroots, industry and governments on standardizing best practice, expanding regulation and investing in education and safeguards. I see this as my duty as an anthropologist who is very invested in communities of people and facilitating expressions of their voice and agency, and who is also actively partnering with governments and big tech to improve policy and infrastructure.

Acknowledgements

This book has been stewing in my brain for a long time. I first took interest in child Influencers in 2010 when undertaking a voluntary internship at *The New Paper*, Singapore Press Holdings. During that time, I was mentored by a very dedicated and kind Assistant Editor, Seto Nu-Wen, who encouraged me to conduct research and pursue stories that uncovered the nuance behind digital cultures. My first newspaper articles on children and their entanglements with social media were published in 2011, and I am ever so grateful to Seto for her guidance in my early years as a researcher.

I am also thankful to all the informants, participants and interviewees who have shared their stories, expertise and time with me throughout my years of fieldwork on child Influencers. Many of these relationships have spanned years, even over a decade, and it is my greatest privilege as an anthropologist to be continually accepted and embraced in your social milieu. Thank you for the rapport, trust and friendship.

I would also like to acknowledge the research funding that has supported this book, especially during a climate where higher education and research are facing a crisis worldwide. A substantial portion of the research for this book was supported by an Australian Research Council Discovery Early Career Researcher Award (DECRA) (DE190100789); the original illustrations were funded by Strategic Research Investment awarded to me by the Faculty of Humanities and Research Office at Curtin University; and the Open Access cost of this book was subsidized by a MCASI Research Small Grant (2024) from the School of Media, Creative Arts and Social Inquiry at Curtin University.

At Polity, I thank Editorial Assistants Stephanie Homer and Maddie Hazelden, and carry lifelong gratitude to Senior Commissioning Editor Mary Savigar for the continued confidence in my writing, our annual rapid-fire brainstorms at conferences around the world, and our friendship over the years.

I also thank the anonymous reviewers of this manuscript whose incisive comments helped to improve the rigour of the writing.

The illustrations were commissioned and directed by me, and created by my wonderful Research Assistant Ardine Keyla – thank you for continuing to be the worm in my brain who can see as I want the world to see. All figures were commissioned by and copyrighted to Crystal Abidin; art was provided by Ardine Keyla. Thank you also to Research Assistant Janey Umback for her help with referencing work.

This book contains some previously published work, for which I would like to thank the publishers and editors for confirming permissions to reuse the materials. Portions of chapter 2 were previously published in 'Preschool stars on YouTube: Child microcelebrities, commercially viable biographies, and interactions with technology', pp. 226–34 in *The Routledge Companion of Children and Digital Media*, edited by Lelia Green, Donell Holloway, Leslie Haddon, Kylie Stevenson and Tama Leaver. London and New York: Routledge. Portions of chapter 3 were previously published in '#familygoals: Family influencers, calibrated amateurism, and justifying young digital labour', *Social Media + Society*

3(2): 1–15. DOI: 10.1177/2056305117707191. Portions of chapter 5 were previously published in 'Child Influencers: How children have become entangled with social media commerce', *Australian Quarterly* 94(3): 3–13. Portions of chapter 10 were previously published in 'Patchwork governance on KidTok: Balancing regulation and community norms', *Policy & Internet* 17(2): 1–14. DOI: 10.1002/poi3.70003.

Earlier versions of the thinking in this book were presented at various events, and I thank the organizers for the invitations to speak and for hosting invigorating Q&A sessions: Australian Influencer Marketing Council (13 February 2024), Digital Child Annual Meeting 2023 by ARC Centre of Excellence for the Digital Child (2 August 2023) and Connecting Ideas WIP Sessions by ARC Centre of Excellence for the Digital Child (19 April 2023). Select portions of the research have also been presented at the Association of Internet Researchers Conference (2024, 2018), the International Communication Association Conference (2024), the Digitizing Early Childhood International Conference (2018) and the Controlling Data Symposium (2016).

At the School of Media, Creative Arts and Social Inquiry (MCASI), I thank Mike Kent, Umberto Ansaldo, Andrew McLean, Cherie Galvin and Lynda Durack for facilitating various funding initiatives that supported this project. At the Research Office at Curtin (ROC), I thank my grant gurus Melanie McKee and Joanne McEwan for being my cheerleaders and critical peers. In the Internet Studies corridor, my heart beams with gratitude to Christina Chau for being my voice of reason and for our million DMs about the balancing act of being working parents. At the ARC Centre of Excellence for the Digital Child, I thank my colleagues in the Connected Node for their collegiality, and especially thank Juliana Zabatiero for being a beacon of light during times of chaos.

Finally, the reality of having two little humans in my life – three, by the time this book is out in the world – is that almost all the writing across the pages of this book was conducted in pockets of time stolen during toddler naps, after bedtime coaxing, or in my most productive witching hour of 0400–0700hrs. For this, I am eternally grateful to Sherman for A+ co-parenting and for being the best human in my entire life. To Acacia and Aspen (and our incubating Pumpkin), I hope you grow up and read this book someday!

Introduction

The scholarship on children and (digital) media is thriving, and thankfully so. Many recent (authored and edited) books focus on the impact of digital technology and devices on children, for instance investigating screen time and tablet use (e.g. Green et al. 2021) or the internet of toys (e.g. Lemish 2022), and still other studies focus on children and how television shapes them, for instance looking at children's TV programmes and TV consumption (e.g. Gunter 2021). More recently, some books are turning to focus on children and social media specifically, studying topics like YouTube as kids' media (e.g. Johnson 2019) and children's performance cultures through digital visual media (e.g. Trezise 2023). Some scholarly (authored and edited) books are also turning to focus on celebrity mummy culture (e.g. Lagerwey 2016), mummy blogs (e.g. Friedman and Calixte 2009) or how women are embracing motherhood alongside digital technologies (e.g. Das 2019) and social media (e.g. Arnold and Martin 2016). This book puts centre stage the 'extremely online' children who were previously supporting cast members in parent-focused digital cultures – Child Influencers.

'Child Influencers' have historically been used as a 'catch-all' term to refer to all forms of children who acquire some form of online celebrity. But as the chapters of this book will demonstrate, the early histories of 'Mummy Bloggers' (chapter 1), 'Micro-Microcelebrity' (chapter 2), 'Family Influencers' (chapter 3), and 'Child Influencers' (chapter 4) indicate that history is much more nuanced. Further, the contemporary discourse on platform-specific phenomena like 'KidTok' (chapter 5), internet-native trends like 'Meme Celebrities' (chapter 6) and 'Viral Stars' (chapter 7), and the legacies of children in traditional entertainment through 'Variety Stars' (chapter 8) underscore that despite not starting out as 'Influencers' per se, many children may go on to parlay or groom their fame into vocational, professional Influencers. More crucially, the wider ecology of institutions and 'Factories' (chapter 9) reveals the increasing structuration of the child Influencer industry involving multiple intermediaries and stakeholders. Finally, followers – including fans and anti-fans/haters – continue to serve as important sources of governance and community policing through their efforts in the 'Ground Zero' (chapter 10) of fan fora and social media. At this juncture, it is helpful to take a step back and consider the larger landscape of 'internet celebrity' as a guide.

Vocabulary and Nuance

In prior work (Abidin 2018), I trace the historical emergence and scholarly conceptualization of 'internet celebrity' to traditional celebrities, ordinary people as celebrities, reality TV celebrities, celebrity–audience relations, DIY celebrity and microcelebrity. We arrive at 'internet celebrity' as the latest iteration of online celebrity. In my body of work, I have stipulated that 'internet celebrities' generally fulfil three criteria:

> *Firstly, internet celebrities are native to the internet.* They are the 'media formats . . . that attain prominence and popu-

larity native to the internet, although the spillover effects and afterlives may include cross-border flows outside of the internet' (Abidin 2018: 15–16). In other words, their fame originates on the internet, and they are 'digital first personalities' (Hutchinson 2019).

Secondly, internet celebrities are mainly known for holding high visibility. However, the morality of their visibility can be attributed to 'fame or infamy, positive or negative attention, talent and skill or otherwise, and whether it be sustained or transient, intentional or by happenstance, monetized or not' (Abidin 2018: 16).

Thirdly, internet celebrities arise from audience interest, which itself is contingent upon personal and cultural preferences. They have to be 'received, watched, and acknowledged by an audience', and as such, the 'success and extent of an internet celebrity's high visibility can vary depending on the platforms they use and the cultural ideologies and tastes of their intended audience' (Abidin 2018: 16).

Going by this framework, internet celebrities is an umbrella term, a catch-all that can comprise all of the 'internet famous' children discussed in this book. However, 'Influencers' are a specific genre of internet celebrity who make concerted decisions about the morality and nature of their visibility. Returning to the attention pairs in the second criterion above, Influencers generally hold high visibility that is attributed to fame, positive attention, talent and skill, and this visibility is usually aimed to be sustained, intentional and monetized (see Abidin 2018: 16). In other words, Influencers are 'vocational, sustained, and highly branded' iterations of internet celebrity (Abidin 2018: 71), the elite, if you will. Correspondingly, 'Child Influencers' are minors and children who feature in the cross-pollinated genres of Influencer cultures, and may at times be referred to via platform-specific terms like 'YouTuber' and 'TikToker', or role-specific terms like 'livestreamer' and 'model'.

In more recent work (Abidin 2025), I detail at length how progressions in internet infrastructure and platform affordances have facilitated the expansion of 'Influencer cultures' to include 'Creator cultures'. In that body of work (chapter 4 in Abidin 2025) I focus especially on how there are distinctive elements to both cultures pertaining to definition, anchor, primary dependent, visibility, relationality, production, value, monetization model and vulnerability risk, and how these correspondingly illuminate the 'nature', 'condition', 'strategy' and 'anticipation' of creator labour differently. For example:

> While Influencers are everyday individuals who *publicize their privacy* to commodify their lifestyles (see Abidin 2015), Creators are users who *create timely contents* to relate to the evolving trends on different platforms.
>
> While Influencers primarily rely on cultivating a persona that is primarily dependent on the *interest of their online communities*, Creators primarily rely on *platformed-supported forms of visibility* – like algorithmic engagement – to maintain connections with viewers.
>
> While Influencers are valuable for their *personal reputation and their ability to foster trust and loyalty* among followers, Creators are valuable for their *ability to navigate platform features and adapt to time-sensitive trends* to foster ongoing visibility with a potential audience.

As such, delineating the origin stories of how different categories of 'internet famous' children come to be is not simply about splitting hairs or about being unnecessarily pedantic. Instead, it helps us understand how and why some 'internet famous' children appear to be more cared for by institutions and jurisdictions, have more access to resources and support, and more equitable opportunities for monetization and career-building than others.

Overview of Chapters

The overview of chapters below offers brief highlights of the genres of 'internet famous' children and the different stakeholders that will be discussed in the book.

Chapter 1 'Mummy Bloggers' focuses on the early origin stories of mummy bloggers in the mid-2000s to early-2010s, as the first instance when babies and very young children became narrated in a public online space. Looking at (archived and/or now defunct) blog platforms, the chapter maps out the original ethos of mummy bloggers (see Arnold and Martin 2016; Das 2019), how they came to partner with brands and clients for endorsements and collaborations (see Lopez 2009), and some of the tensions that these early mummy bloggers were navigating between their personal ethos, shared community norms and the prospect of additional income (see Lehto 2020; Orton-Johnson 2017). The early genesis of mummy blogging was a milestone moment where the previously undervalued feminine/maternal knowledge and labour around childcare was recognized, valued and compensated for by brands for the first time, and the presence of children in commercial blogging was important for instilling reader confidence and blogger reputation. Case studies include early mummy bloggers and later iterations of them – Yummy Mummies, Tradwives and Beige Mums – on platforms including Instagram, TikTok and YouTube, who are included pseudonymously.

Chapter 2 'Micro-Microcelebrity' traces the emergence of micro-microcelebrities – the children of microcelebrities who attain online fame through proximate micro-celebrification and repeated exposure to the public – and their early pathways to monetizing opportunities. In other words, we look at extreme forms of sharenting (see Blum-Ross 2015; Blum-Ross and Livingstone 2017) to understand how and why some parents neglect their children's rights to be forgotten (see Haley 2020) and wander into the risks of datafying their children (see Siibak and Traks 2019) to groom public portfolios for them. Looking more closely at Instagram, the chapter considers milestones and strategies like pregnancy announcements, pre-birth social media handle reservations, brand tie-ups from conception to birth, personalized merchandise, birth announcements and similar. Notably, the first discrete digital footprints, social media accounts and digital estates for the children of Influencers were essential for these women to transition across topical genres (from lifestyle, fashion, F&B towards parenting, childcare, education and the like), and expand their availability to a wider genre of potential advertisers. Further, the public profiles of these micro-microcelebrities became important sites where difficult conversations about the stigma of unwed pregnancies/pro-life decisions, young parenthood/teen mothers and single parents/financial precarity unfolded, with the children emerging as symbols for the public affect and discourse. Case studies include the children of Influencer pioneers and their children.

Chapter 3 'Family Influencers' looks at families who have turned themselves into social media content creators in the family genre, taking to daily vlogging, staged events and activities, and highly parasocial filming strategies to establish themselves as Influencers while capitalizing on audience interest among everyday, ordinary people (see Turner 2010). Looking specifically at YouTube, the chapter traces the origins of family Influencers to reality TV families who accumulate fame for being extraordinary, exotic and/or eccentric, as forms of identity-making specifically for commercially viable ends (see Kennedy 2024). The chapter will demonstrate the concept of 'anchor' and 'filler' content, which family Influencers use to maintain the professionalism of their content while sustaining impressions of intimacy, and expand on the theory of 'calibrated amateurism' (see Abidin 2017a), which explains how authenticity is strategized and performed as an anticipatory mitigation of accusations against the parents. While some aspects of how family Influencer content is structured is made more visible, other parts are made more obscure. With filler and behind-the-scenes content often framed through humour and playfulness, and the workplace and home environment becoming permanently conflated, the boundaries between 'work' and 'play' become difficult to differentiate. Case studies include Canadian Eh Bee Family, American Reality Changers and Singaporean Jebbey Family.

Chapter 4 'Child Influencers' interrogates child Influencers as a cross-pollinated genre of Influencer cultures where the main actors are minors. In many instances, children across the various streams of online fame (chapters 1–8) eventually become child Influencers. Looking closely at YouTube and a handful of other platforms, the chapter considers a brief overview of the changing context of child Influencer content genres, target audiences, age-based monetization activity and parasocial relationships across platforms. The chapter will provide a framework for how we can ask meaningful questions about why we should and how we can be concerned about this growing industry vertical, and what the tensions between the terms 'Influencer' and 'creator' signal in terms of platform, parental and policy responsibilities in light of recent government regulations worldwide (see Kilkenny 2024; Kumar 2020; Rieffel 2023; UK Parliament 2021, 2022). Case studies include prominent child Influencers, who will be discussed pseudonymously, as well as prominent K-pop cover artists Deksorkrao from Thailand, child model Niuniu from China and child YouTuber Ryan from the US.

Chapter 5 'KidTok' studies the phenomenon of children who accumulate online fame on TikTok. In focusing specifically on TikTok, the chapter presents a survey of different 'extents' of online fame attached to children on the platform, and offers a framework for the possible entry and exit routes to the condition of being 'TikTok famous' (see Turvy and Abidin 2025). The rapid uptake and mainstreaming of TikTok during the very short span of the 'pandemic years' has inevitably led to an explosion of content almost entirely anchored on minors in the privacy of their homes, in schools and in other 'third spaces' (see Oldenburg 1999). It also demonstrates the savvy of TikTokers in harnessing algorithmic visibility as valuable digital labour to support fellow creators on the platform (see Maris et al. 2024). While this may be an important avenue for community building, and for parents/guardians and young people to connect with each other, the pandemic years on TikTok have pivoted the conversation about children and social media to focus on presence, agency and empowerment. This case study-heavy chapter will include the 'Maia Knight Twins' and their pivot towards enforced privacy, the 'Pandemic Babies' trend and 'Four Seasons Baby' meme as instances of proliferating conspiracy theories, and the '#ImJustAKid' challenge which presents a more wholesome iteration of KidTok phenomena.

Chapter 6 'Meme Celebrities' focuses on 'meme celebrities' who are 'ordinary people (unwittingly) captured under compromising circumstances with notable expressions or gestures and become iconized as memes' (see Abidin 2018: 44). Meme celebrities are very often young children, whose image is taken out of context, and whose likeness becomes a shorthand to express a specific emotion or situation in internet discourse. Looking closely at various social media platforms, including messaging platforms across the Asia Pacific region which have features that enable personalized stickers, the chapter offers a critique of meme celebrity culture when the children and their guardians have little agency in offering a backstory to the image. Drawing on the legacy of memes as highly communal phenomena (see Phillips 2016; Shifman 2013) with potential participatory politics (see Milber 2018; Mina 2019), the chapter also considers the consequences of merchandising meme cultures, where third parties profit off the image of these children. Case studies include 'Jinmiran baby' of messaging sticker meme fame, Gavin Mastodon of 'The Internet's Son' fame, and the brothers of viral YouTube video 'Charlie Bit My Finger'.

Chapter 7 'Viral Stars' traces the phenomenon of viral stars, usually comprising children who become trending content and wildly popular among global audiences within a very short span of time. Surveying various social media platforms and their entanglements with the television talk show circuit, the chapter argues that these children are 'everyday users in organically viral social media posts, especially those involving young children and teenagers, [who] become systemically absorbed, groomed, and even exploited by the mainstream media into traditional celebrity icons' (Abidin 2018: 56). The chapter ties in concepts from media studies scholarship, such as the 'money shot' (Grindstaff 2002), which zooms in on an apparent act of emotional vulnerability that goes on to become iconized to capture audience attention. The chapter will also consider how television talk show circuits are involved in the production of such viral star moments, through social media challenges issued by nighttime talk shows. A detailed case study focuses on Sophia Grace & Rosie of 'Nicki Minaj cover' fame, and a brief case study of Park Geon Roung, the 'Baby Shark' boy, considers how child viral stars might be differently managed under different institutions and jurisdictions in the South Korean market.

Chapter 8 'Variety Stars' looks at the child 'variety stars' in the Korean entertainment industry, against the backdrop of a fast-growing industry that has quickly leveraged social media publicity and fandoms. Specifically, this case study-heavy chapter focuses on two shows to elucidate important concepts: *The Return of Superman* (TROS), a variety reality TV show launched in September 2013 by the Korean Broadcasting System (KBS) network which documents 'a day in the life' of male South

Korean celebrities who become primary caregivers for their young children over forty-eight-hour periods; and *Half-Moon Friends* (HMF), a limited-run variety reality TV show launched April 2016, featuring K-pop idol group WINNER running a daycare for ten children over two weeks. The entanglement of the TROS fandom on social media has resulted in very intense online curations of these children's images, while the popularity of the HMF children has resulted in several more years of off-screen friendships and collaborations with the K-pop artists, including the afterlives as child and family Influencers. In all, the chapter provides new ways of thinking about how fame flows between the traditional entertainment industry, social media industries and Influencer industry.

Chapter 9 'Factories' provides a top-level overview of the types of institutions, structures and systems that come to sustain the ecologies of children's online fame. Through traditional and digital ethnographic methods and personal interviews, the chapter considers the role of Influencer agencies, talent incubators, managerial intermediaries and the creator partnership programmes of various platforms in facilitating the continuous growth and intensification of the celebritization and subsequent commodification of childhood online. Looking specifically at the South Korean context – to build on some of my recent work on children as K-pop trainees (Lee and Abidin 2023) and child idols (Lee et al. 2024) – I consider in depth the case study of Korean-American child model Ella Gross, who has operated across the social media, child modelling, K-pop entertainment and child Influencer industries for over a decade.

Finally, *Chapter 10 'Ground Zero'* interrogates online fora and watchful lurkers as forms of 'lateral surveillance' (Andrejevic 2002; Reeves 2012), who serve as an important source of policing child Influencer activity through the concept of 'ground zero'. Traditionally, ground zero is understood as the starting point of an activity, or the homebase for a group to congregate. But it also refers to the point exactly below where a bomb might have been activated – an origin story, a trigger of flurried activity, a harbinger of chaos, so to speak. Looking closely at Reddit and other pseudonymous online fora, in this chapter we systematically study networks of online discussion threads focused specifically on the 'Wren Eleanor scandal' as a case study to provide a framework of 'community governance' (Turvy and Abidin 2025). These include 'snark' fora on mummy bloggers, parenting Influencers, child celebrities and the like. While at once appearing as mere gossip, these sites are often the ground zero for breaking news regarding the violation of children's rights, the mistreatment or abuse of 'internet famous' children, and other nuanced discussions and debates about the role of parents in managing children's online fame.

Collectively, the chapters aim to consolidate various theories and frameworks on 'internet famous' children; provide a comprehensive overview of the various histories, genres and socio-cultural contexts that have led to the entanglement of ordinary children with circuits of online fame; and share new fieldwork and established case studies to enhance these concepts and frameworks through original empirical data from across the Asia Pacific region, and across various digital platforms. Readers can expect to access an intersection of ideas from an interdisciplinary and inter-field perspective, including celebrity studies, Influencer studies, children and the media studies. The case studies also aim to challenge some of the oft-quoted (and usually Anglo-centric, middle-classed) moral panics against the visibility of children on social media, or in the media more broadly. The text gives voice and agency to the children, their parents and guardians, and the agents and managers who have been striving to improve the child Influencer market through their everyday practices and community norms.

Suggestions for Reading

This book has been intentionally positioned to be an accessible primer that appeals to both a generic non-specialist audience and scholarly experts. While the chapters are designed to be read discretely, here I provide some suggestions for how students may want to group some chapters to glean a more macro picture of the phenomenon.

To read the book in two blocks: chapters 1 to 8 focus on *pathways and pivots*. Each chapter covers a specific genre or field of child online fame, and underscores a framework, theory or concept. Chapters 9 to 10 focus on *provocations*. They highlight some critical implications of online fame for children, potential consequences, mitigation strategies from various stakeholders and grassroots reactions.

To read the book in three blocks: chapters 1 to 5 are organized by the *chronological emergence of each genre* (i.e. mummy bloggers late-2000s, micro-microcelebrity early-2010s, family Influencers mid-2010s, child Influencers mid-2010s, KidTok late-2010s), and how the child in each of these genres is shifting towards being (perceived as) an independent actor. Chapters 6 to 8 are organized by *mainstream familiarity* (for the imagined 'Global North' reader), as all three markets (i.e. meme celebrities, viral stars, variety stars) have been long established in East Asian markets since the 2000s, but are only just gaining popularity worldwide as knowledge of the 'production pipeline' of child Influencers is becoming mainstream. Chapters 9 to 10 are organized from *macro to micro* actors in the Influencer ecology (i.e. agencies and incubators in industry, users in internet forums).

A Brief Note on Methods and Ethical Decisions

The data in this book are based on longitudinal ethnographic research spanning 2008 to 2024. The methodology/methods primarily comprise traditional ethnography, digital ethnography, personal interviews, content analysis and document analysis. Evidence of these scholarly methods can be viewed in my body of published work searchable online. The methodological decisions underpinning this anthropological study have adopted a decolonial approach, but discussions of decolonial theory and frameworks are for another occasion.

The case studies are referenced via a mixture of real names, social media monikers, pseudonyms and anonymity. The primary methodology of this book is traditional and digital ethnography. It is for this reason that some of the stories shared within are very personal anecdotes solicited based on informant rapport and trust in my role as an anthropologist. As such, I have made executive decisions regarding the identification and naming of some informants regardless of their full consent to be identified and named in academic writing. In instances where the case studies reflect negatively on the children, such as discussions on controversy and scandal, I have elected to either (1) discuss only the most prolific of these examples that are already mainstream in the international media, or (2) discuss the examples pseudonymously or anonymously after applying creative 'fabrication as an ethical practice' (Markham 2012). This protects the case studies that are not (yet) mainstream from over-exposure while maintaining the ethnographic fidelity of the nuance I want to demonstrate. These pseudonymous and anonymous case studies are drawn from a series of projects investigating the life course and genres of Influencers spanning Southeast Asia (2008–), Australasia (2011–), the Nordic countries (2014–) and the Asia Pacific region, with a special focus on East Asia (2019–).

While many of the informants whom I have personally interviewed and interacted with over the years have given me permission to study and use the images of their child, I have elected to exclude any screengrabs of actual children in this book after contemplating the longevity of print media. Instead, I use line drawings to elucidate and visualize the scenes I portray.

Please note that I capitalize the use of 'Influencer' when referring to these individuals via their vocation or in their capacity as professionals, in contrast to deploying 'influencer' as a concept most popularized in marketing research.

1

Mummy Bloggers

Introduction

Mummy bloggers are among the pioneers in what would eventually evolve into the Influencer industry today. While the earliest of them began their profiles and personae on blogs as diary or review writers, as digital cultures progressed and new platforms emerged, later evolutions of mummy bloggers focused on other media like images (for instance on Instagram), short videos (for instance on TikTok) or long videos (for instance on YouTube). When the formats began to pivot to visual cultures, it seemed like the barriers to entry were lowered, and the market rapidly expanded. The competitive nature of ever-changing visual cultures also saw the rise and fall of trends every few months, enticing these later mummy bloggers to constantly update their content styles, aesthetic choices and narrative disclosure to maintain an interested audience. Although the original ethos of mothering on social media focused on negotiations of motherhood and its associated rewards and challenges (Arnold and Martin 2016; Das 2019), somewhere along the way, we began to focus less and less on the origin stories of mummy bloggers who once upon a time strived to challenge the status quo to represent and present maternal knowledge and labour as productive and valuable.

Communication studies scholar Lori Kido Lopez studied the 2005 BlogHer conference in California, where over 300 attendees gathered to 'shatter the stigma' that women in the blog community 'only wrote about children in their weblogs', instead offering that they were also 'businesswomen, politicians, and cultural commentators' (Lopez 2009: 730). She offers a feminist take that 'mummy bloggers' present ways to 'challeng[e] and reinterpre[t] representations of motherhood' (2009: 730) as consumers and through community. This angle points to the myriad roles, functions and responsibilities that mothers take on, juggling multiple skillsets at once, and mummy blogs were the spaces where these practices could be narrated, neatly documented, discursively studied, seamlessly shared and consequently appraised.

Despite being one of the earliest studies on mummy blogs, the conflict that Lopez recounts at the 2005 conference continues to this day. Even within the mummy blogging genre per se, researchers have found instances of 'combative mothering' where there is 'constant competition' around their various 'parenting philosophies, practices, and choices' (Abetz and Moore 2018: 265). Media studies scholar Mari Lehto's (2020) study of 'bad motherhood' on Finnish mummy blogs found evidence of these women teasing out the contemporary challenges of parenting, including the need to 'dismantle the myth of the perfect mother' to expand conversations about what constitutes 'normative' mothering.

In more recent scholarship, a review of studies on parent Influencers asserts that the body of work tends to disproportionately focus on mothers and discourses on motherhood, and does not often consider the conceptualization of parental wellbeing (Beuckels and De Wolf 2024). A more longitudinal connection to the early origins of mummy bloggers, as this chapter offers, tells us why this is precisely the case. Despite tensions in the genre that have now spanned decades, two things remain constant. Firstly, mummy blogs and later Influencers who still identify with the genre focus specifically on mothers (rather than their children per se), to network, commiserate, strategize, share the ups and downs about parenthood (Orton-Johnson 2017). Secondly, while mummy blogging did not initially begin as a monetized endeavour, this changed when blogs became popular and mummy bloggers were targeted by advertisers to engage in paid reviews and sponsored advertorials (Hunter 2016); in other words, it is important to remember that the early genesis of mummy blogs were among the first examples of when the previously under-valued maternal knowledge and skillsets required to bring up a child and maintain a household were assigned a literal dollar value, which was empowering for many women. As such, this chapter considers iterations of mummy bloggers through the first generation of 'Mummy Bloggers' on blogs where discourse focused on feminism and self-care, and how this has evolved through more contemporary iterations: 'Yummy Mummies' who preach consumerist luxury and ecological disavowal on Instagram; 'Tradwives' who espouse traditional gender roles in line with Christian fundamentalist beliefs on TikTok; and 'Beige Mums' who lean into Instagrammability and an ecological ethos in their aesthetic and businesses.

'Mummy Bloggers': The First Generation

It is 2011. I have the pleasure of visiting the home of one of the first-generation mummy bloggers in Singapore for a sit-down interview. Thirty-two-year-old Elaine greets me at the door of her apartment in a private condominium estate, and the moment my shoes are off she ushers me towards her store-room of 'samples'. It is important to emphasize that Elaine was not receiving remuneration for these goods and writing reviews of them on her blog – after all, she had a full-time job in the corporate sector and was not allowed to moonlight. Some of these samples were predictable: children's clothes and shoes, books and toys and even education DVDs. But Elaine has also received offers to 'sample' an expensive stroller and provide her honest assessment to the 500 viewers who visit her blog daily. This might seem like a small number, but it is 2011, where only half of the country's population of 5 million people used social networks (Kemp 2011), and where top mummy bloggers in the Southeast Asian region were averaging 1,000 daily views. Mummy bloggers were only just springing into mainstream popularity, following the early wave of political blogs and teen lifestyle vlogs that had been emerging in the last five years or so.

Her only child is three-year-old Edwin, who is home with us. It is a weekday, and Elaine has taken personal leave from her workplace for us to conduct this interview in her home. She tells me that most of her readers are 'working mums' themselves who may not always have the time to 'study' and 'research' the things they buy for their children, and because she gives her 'honest opinion' and is 'practical' about the utility of the samples as a 'working mum' herself, there is easy rapport and trust between them. On her blog, Elaine's product reviews are often accompanied by photographs of her 'testing the goods'. She makes it a point to include her face in all the photos to assure readers that she is not simply 'recycling stock photos' provided by the companies. This is part of her feminist ethos of authenticity, in wanting readers to know she is an active and involved parent, to challenge the normative discourse (see Lopez 2009) of disinterested working mothers in Singapore who would usually 'outsource' parenting to live-in domestic workers.

As our interview unfolds, she tells me that these days brands are asking her to pivot to 'mummy self-care' and she is sent

Figure 1.1. Artist impression of first-generation mummy blogs.

samples of cleansing foams and cooling facial gels. The PR emails ask if she could please continue to focus on her child but include small narrations about how their products 'benefit mums'. We muse about how facial cleansers were, after all, 'universal', and having to brand one as being 'great for mums' was a bit of a stretch. Elaine posted a review, but declined the ask to sell the cleanser as being 'for mums', as she did not feel that using her mummy blogging platform to promote unrelated products was in line with the parenting philosophies she had been espousing (see Abetz and Moore 2018). Like many of the early mummy bloggers discussed in the scholarship above, it was important to Elaine to not appear as if she was 'selling out' or opportunistically genre-hopping to include an ever-expanding repertoire of product and service recommendations.

Our conversation is interrupted because Edwin, who has been weaving in and out of the living room where we were, wants to show me his bedroom. Elaine takes me on a house tour, but Edwin quickly loses interest in me and returns to the living room where his play corner is. A few moments of casual chat later, Elaine and I make our way down the corridor towards the living room. I follow her lead, until she pauses to peek around the corner to 'spy' on Edwin. He is playing with a new toy – a sample from a 'new client'. Elaine then explains that she would usually observe her son 'interacting' with the sample toys and books, noting whether they appear 'self-explanatory' or intuitive and whether they are age-appropriate. She is cognizant of needing to witness Edwin in 'his natural habitat' to get an honest gauge of the product, and we both joke that it sounds like she is filming a nature documentary. Her emphasis on allowing Edwin to be 'in situ' occurs to me as a preemptive pushback against potential accusations of 'bad mothering' (Lehto 2020), of appearing negligent and allowing toys and devices to parent in proxy, or of appearing as if she was pressuring her son into becoming a guinea pig for these products. Elaine grabs her small camera from the bedroom and snaps a few photos of Edwin playing with the toy. She tells me that, later tonight, she will transfer the photo to her laptop and write up the blogpost, following her observations of Edwin's 'live demonstration'.

By this point, Edwin is noticeably distracted by the camera and no longer wants to play. With muscle memory, Elaine sits herself down on the playmat, scoops Edwin into her lap, holds up the toy for him to play with, hollers for her live-in domestic helper to give them a hand, passes her the camera, and gets a few shots of mother-and-son. Collectively, the helper and I coo and caw to get Edwin's attention and instantly 'bond' over our instincts. I half-joke that she makes for a 'very good assistant', given her sleight of hand. She tells me that she is used to helping, and that it is 'quite fun to help madam for the blog'. It seems like a family activity.

'Yummy Mummy': Luxury Motherhood on Instagram

'Yummy mummy' is popular slang to describe mothers who still appear attractive post-childbirth, operating under the stereotype that women's appearance and wellbeing are not upkept post-partum. More crucially, the stereotype implies that mothers can still be sexually attractive in the dating market, still be well groomed, still prioritize self-care, and still have time for the 'holy trio' of gym time, salads and lattes. Originally deployed as a compliment, the yummy mummy was popularized by celebrity mothers from the traditional entertainment industry, including through the 'autobiographical guidebook[s] on pregnancy and motherhood' authored by these women (Littler 2013: 227).

On closer inspection, 'yummy mummies' are often pitted in opposition to the 'working mums' mentioned earlier, simply because these women have the privilege to opt out of work altogether. The stereotype extends to offer that yummy mummies regularly engage in very privileged forms of consumption comprising designer prams, branded baby wear and expensive baby toys, while being clad in luxury goods themselves. To afford the time and effort that goes into this appearance maintenance, they usually also have hired help. During my fieldwork, I once encountered a yummy mummy in her mid-twenties who had three live-in domestic helpers: one to nanny her kindergartener, one to nanny her toddler and one to maintain her household. She regularly travels on business class with her children in tow and her helpers on economy.

Like mummy bloggers, some yummy mummies also engage in monetized content production even if many of them do not need to do so, or do so as a mere hobby. As an extreme iteration of first-generation mummy bloggers, studies on advertising find that the discourse deployed by yummy mummy advertisements tends to use animosity and envy to stimulate aspiration and desire, and brand motherhood as almost exclusively

Figure 1.2. Artist impression of 'yummy mummies' and 'luxury mums' on Instagram.

focused on glamour (O'Donohoe 2006). As with all cultures and genres, some things are taken to the extreme.

Between 2017 to 2019, a popular reality TV series *Yummy Mummies* was produced by Australian network 7plus. The show was widely watched (and hated) by viewers worldwide after it was licensed on Netflix. In twenty episodes across two seasons, a group of lavish expectant mothers are seen taking the yummy mummy stereotype to the extreme, as the show documented their lifestyles and antics. Several of the main plots focused on discussions and beliefs about breastfeeding (not wanting to 'damage' their breasts, perceiving breastfeeding as 'gross', acceding to breastfeeding as long as they are promised a 'mummy makeover' thereafter); birth plans (being 'too posh to push', electing for c-sections to 'preserve' their vaginas, considering surrogates as an 'easier' option); and shopping lists of lavish 'push presents'. Dozens of discussion forums and tens of thousands of livetweets later, viewers generally agreed that while the show was 'tacky', they could not help but 'hate watch' it for entertainment value. By this point, while self-identifying as a 'yummy mummy' was usually intended to be a compliment, it was instead often perceived by audiences with cynicism, and deployed by haters as criticism or an insult.

In the scholarship, the 'yummy mummy' has been studied in contemporary British (Littler 2013), North American (Anderson et al. 2014), Australian (Malatzky 2017) and Danish cultures (Prinds et al. 2020), each reflecting how societal norms and values about class and motherhood shape different iterations of the stereotype and their implications on local mothers. It is unanimous that yummy mummies are overtly sexualized and generally from the upper-middle class, and very privileged. The discourse also sees yummy mummies subject to 'infantilization' (Littler 2013: 233–5), as evidenced by the frequent tantrums sighted on the reality show.

The excessive and luxurious behaviours of yummy mummies is what cultural studies scholar Jo Littler (2013: 235) has identified as an 'ecological disavowal': no need to labour over organic foods when fast and easy options are fine; no need to consider the wider structural consequences and considerations for the environment when consumption is necessary to sustain this lifestyle. Some scholars argue that the yummy mummy discourse ultimately points to a 'neoliberal crisis of the home', reflecting 'longer work hours, the erosion of collective supports and heightened consumption expectations' (Anderson et al. 2014: 95). Indeed, some mothers who buy into the 'yummy mummy' ideal are reflexive about their internal conflict arising from the tensions between this discourse of self-care, as compared to other ideals about good mothering, but ultimately they are not offered many other alternate scripts to draw on (Malatzky 2017). Tongue-in-cheek commentaries about the trend offer alternatives like 'scummy mummy' and 'slummy mummy' (Rodie 2017) as options to reflect the real-life mess that comes with mothering. On an individual level, research has also found that the 'yummy mummy' discourse reveals how while women 'felt strengthened through motherhood', their experience with post-partum bodies left them dissatisfied and 'yummy mummy' stereotypes provided a small allowance to reconcile these tensions (Prinds et al. 2020: 266).

On balance, the scholarship and public discourse agree that the 'yummy mummy' discourse is in some ways about 'mum shaming' and pitting mothers against each other for the various pregnancy, childbirth and parenting decisions they make for a plethora of reasons. However, it is important to underscore that much of the criticism of yummy mummies sidesteps conversations about class and privilege, and their intersections with race and Whiteness. In a similar vein, this is a topic that the 'Tradwives' on TikTok seem to tiptoe around.

'Tradwives': Gender Roles on TikTok

The early-2020s saw the rise of 'Tradwives' trending on TikTok. The aesthetic primarily sees apron-clad women in cottagecore dresses and freshly coiled hair, minding their equally well-dressed children, who are usually in matching clothes, at home. The content sees the women in those very same outfits seamlessly weaving through the kitchen engaged in a range of domestic chores, especially focused on baking and cooking from scratch, and minding their brood of children usually with homeschooling and home-based religious education. Their beliefs are contingent upon being stay-at-home mums where their rightful place is, submitting to their sole breadwinner husbands, and enforcing traditional gender roles in the home. Their politics are often hidden from view, but solidly rooted in the traditional Christian fundamentalist movement, American

Figure 1.3. Artist impression of 'tradwives' making food from scratch on TikTok.

conservatism and right-wing values, which are often opposed to modern-day feminism.

Tradwives became mainstream online during the pandemic, where prolonged periods of home-based self-isolation around the world saw everyday people and Influencers pivoting to the domestic locus of the home to produce content, even glamourizing the 'domestic toil of homemakers' (*The Economist* 2024). It is in this climate that the 'romanticized depictions of domestic work' pervaded TikTok, and 'espouse[d] a romantic ideal of feminine domesticity as an escape from the "double shift" [which] represents a backlash to popular feminism's failed injunction to "lean in"' (Sykes 2024: 1). A 2022 news article describes tradwives as a 'niche subculture' that includes women who are fond of the aesthetic and some of the values, but who may not subscribe entirely to the politics (Kaur 2022).

But its mainstreaming, and the subsequent masking of tradwife values and politics under the guise of being a mere aesthetic and lifestyle, has enabled right-wing groups to adopt and usurp the subculture for ideology dissemination. Newer scholarship aptly describes tradwives as 'communities of right-wing women who commercialize social media to commodify traditional heteronormative renditions of femininity that are equal parts ideology and aesthetic' (Sykes and Hopner 2024: 453). In a nutshell, the scholarship surmises tradwives as an exemplar of 'far right women influencers' (Leidig 2023) who aim to 'soften and normalize white supremacy' (Love 2020: 1), by presenting their lifestyles as a 'timeless, abstract ideal and a practical lifestyle hack' (Deem 2023: 4), when in reality their 'nostalgic (white) femininity [is] tied to locally specific cultural histories' (Mattheis 2021: 91). So while tradwives may not customarily advertise products and services as per first-generation mummy bloggers or the yummy mummies of Instagram, they peddle in the sale of politics and ideology through the parasocial and communicative strategies long established in Influencer cultures.

'Beige Mums': 24/7 Aesthetics on YouTube

Influencer Sarah pivoted to becoming a beige mum in her thirties, after she left her job as a teacher to be a full-time Influencer and to care for her two children at home. This also coincided with the new home she purchased and renovated with her spouse, which was decorated in every shade of beige and brown possible. It is as if her house exists in a perpetual

Figure 1.4. Artist impression of 'beige mums' styling their home decor and children's outfits in the 'beige aesthetic' on TikTok.

brown tint in real life. She dresses only in neutral colours like white and beige, and her children are always clad similarly in matching clothes. Even her husband is seen in photographs in the same hues, with the occasional exception of some black pants. Likewise, the decor on the shelves that she reveals on Instagram bears only neutral-coloured items, and her children's toys are mostly made of wood and neutral linen fabric.

Because Sarah began her career as a lifestyle Influencer in her twenties and would often demonstrate her fashion sense through beautiful outfits and luxury handbags, longtime followers were seen questioning her sudden turnaround to being a 'beige mum': 'Your whole house is brown? What's happening?', 'Can your poor kids even see colour?', 'Do you just bleach all your clothes to match?' Other cheeky followers are often seen chiming in to clarify that Sarah had progressed from 'beige' to 'light beige' to 'dark beige'. But still, there were other more serious commenters debating whether her wallpaper was 'desert sand', or 'autumn sunset', or 'rust' as they wanted to emulate her style.

I got to meet with Sarah at an event, and after building initial rapport asked her about being a 'beige mum'. She explains that her aesthetic was really about making her job and her life 'easier':

> My job involves documenting my life all the time, and my content mostly focuses on my home. It makes life easier when everything is neat and tidy, but also aesthetically pleasing, so I don't have to spend extra time and effort to [stage] my house every time I want to take a photo or film a video. Every corner of my house is always 'camera-ready'. It really saves me a lot of time and effort.

In other words, the plain palette of her household is meant to maximize the 'Instagrammability' of Sarah's domestic space which doubles up as her workplace. Sarah tells me that she was inspired by the 'Japandi' – Japan-Scandinavian – aesthetic of minimalism and muted interior design. And although in online videos and posts she often responds to queries about her home decor as being 'Japandi-inspired' or 'Japandi style', the reality is that most of her homewares were purchased from the Chinese e-commerce platform Taobao. Sarah simply had an expert eye for curating goods, and rebranding them with her interior design skills and narrative branding. Despite the mass-produced origins of her homewares, Sarah insists that she makes environmentally-conscious decisions by selecting wood, metals and other natural materials over harmful materials like plastic, to reduce environmental degradation.

News reports and satirical commentaries describe the 'sad beige mum' as 'a woman determined to keep the garish implements of childhood at bay, and instead foster a sober palette of beige-on-beige' (McCusker 2025). Beige mums are often subject to online hate for their 'neutral nurseries and toys' (McLaughlin 2024). Followers criticize them for their 'colourless toys and clothing' (Nicioli 2024). In fact, much of the commentary on discussion forums has even gone so far as to accuse beige mums of child abuse, for depriving their children of 'proper development' or 'joy'. Some jest that these actions may cultivate 'colour blindness' in their children. This chatter led to at least one news article featuring a child development expert to clarify that 'relational development' rather than 'materialistic objects' will have more of an impact on children's development (Nicioli 2024), and that the 'beige mum' aesthetic is harmless. But for Sarah, it goes beyond that.

Like many beige mums, Sarah's contents substantially focus on making ecological decisions for her family – a stark contrast to the 'ecological disavowal' (Littler 2013: 235) practised by the yummy mummies discussed earlier. She often gives followers recommendations of organic foods, low-waste kitchen products, and tips for making natural soap and cleansing liquids in her home organization tutorials on YouTube. She also has a small online stall where she imports and sells linen and natural cotton clothes for children, and wooden trinkets and toys.

Conclusion

As I close this chapter, I think back on all the mummy bloggers I have interviewed in the past years, and realize that all of them who identified with this genre focused their contents on themselves as mothers and on motherhood as a journey. I try to recall if I would recognize the children of these mummy bloggers if I ever saw them on the street, but realize that the children were only occasionally photographed and not often the focus of the discourse. But the next iteration of parents who groom 'micro-microcelebrities' would soon usurp these norms as they place their very young children front and centre in their branding.

2

Micro-Microcelebrity

Introduction

I first started following Influencers via their early iteration as bloggers in 2005, and began to seriously study them in 2007/8. By the mid-2010s, some of the first cohort of young Influencers began to transit through life stages like marriage, homemaking and pregnancies – including teen pregnancies, premarital babies, separation and single mum journeys – and their contents began to pivot away from lifestyle more generally to parenting more specifically. To be even more precise, unlike the mummy bloggers, yummy mummies, tradwives and beige mums discussed in the previous chapter, some of these Influencer mothers framed their contents to centre almost entirely on their very young children. In prior work, I referred to these children as 'micro-microcelebrities', whose fame is cultivated through a 'more prolific, deliberate, and commercial form' (Abidin 2015) of 'sharenting'.

In one of the earliest pieces of work on the phenomenon, tech policy scholar Alicia Blum-Ross (2015) reflects on sharenting as the act of parents sharing images and stories about their children on social networking sites, resulting in a plethora of digital footprints. For children of Influencers, this is all the more concerning as the digital footprints that accumulate in the very many public spaces where their childhoods are documented – often without their consent – revoke their right to be forgotten (Haley 2020). But some parents who 'sharent' are keenly aware of the ethical dilemmas of their practice, at once acknowledging its importance in constructing their self-identities while noting that their exposed children bear some risks (Blum-Ross and Livingstone 2017). In their review of the scholarship, media studies scholar Andra Siibak and communication management scholar Keily Traks suggest that sharenting offers distant family and friends the opportunity to be involved in the upbringing of children, and is also an important outlet for parents to garner support and advice on their parenting journey (Siibak and Traks 2019). However, they also surmise that the dominant concerns regarding the 'dark sides' of sharenting include 'the emergence of a datafied child', the 'loss of privacy' and 'potential distress' to the relationship between parents and their children (Siibak and Traks 2019: 115).

Yet, micro-microcelebrity continues to persist as a form of extreme sharenting, for it is a lucrative commercial strategy. Scholars who remind us to consider the ethics of child-created contents tell us that these are sites for 'discursively codifying particular articulations of concepts such as family to reinforce purchasing and marketing norms' (Burroughs and Feller 2021: 217). For many of the Influencer mothers whom I have interviewed across close to two decades in Southeast Asia, East Asia and the Nordic countries, this was exactly their intention, as the extension of their previously parent-centred mummy blogger contents to child-centred contents was perceived as a natural evolution of their business. In this chapter, we consider the various rationales and strategies by parents who engage in micro-microcelebrity, considering instances where sharenting is a necessary strategy for pivoting their personal brand, the process of proximate micro-celebrification, and the process of debuting digital estates, but also the issues when fandoms form around the baby and when very young children appear to be utilized as props in advertising, resulting in the overt commodification of their childhood (Hudders et al. 2024).

Sharenting as Branding Pivot

One Influencer I interviewed over four years was in her late teens when she announced her surprise pregnancy in a YouTube video, followed by the launch of a blogpost documenting her shotgun wedding that took place shortly after. Her career was doing very well and she did not intend to pursue further studies in university. In other words, she wanted to continue her Influencer business, teen pregnancy and all. Thus, to resolve the risk of unwanted exposure or gossip, she opted to make her pregnancy and quick marriage public, to be 'accountable and transparent' to the over 1.5 million followers she had across all her platforms. She tells me:

> I'd rather be true to myself and honest to my followers, and this will help push back on some of the gossip. When they can see that I am being very real about my struggles and my journey, I'm sure they will support me . . . of course there will be haters, I can't control that . . . but I'm not doing anything shameful, I am taking responsibility.

In subsequent interviews in more casual settings, the then young mother tells me that debuting her child online was a calculated move for her to continue to maintain sponsorship and endorsement opportunities. While some brands shied away from her for fear of backlash from customers, she now also received a much wider variety and higher volume of proposals and offers for brands who could now partner with her to promote parenting and baby products.

Another Influencer who has had a similar trajectory tells me that she places her children front and centre of her content to control the public exposure surrounding them. She was in her early twenties when she had her son, but was unmarried and raising him as a single mother:

> I know I have a lot of new followers who only [recently subscribed to me] because they heard about my unwed pregnancy – I'm not stupid, I know this, I read the forums and I see the Google search trends and people also just tell this to me outrightly. And since they are so curious about my son, I'll show them pictures of him. You don't have to dig into my life. But more importantly, I can control what I am showing, when I want to do it, how I want to do it, rather than have people dox me. If you 'feed' them [the followers searching for pictures of her son], they won't be so desperate.

She confesses that while she sometimes uses images of her son to 'attract reader attention' so that views on her sponsored Instagram posts are boosted, she also uses the opportunity to start difficult conversations:

> I hope that when they see my son they can stop and think about who they are hating on. What did this innocent baby do to you? . . . But not everyone is like that. Sometimes people tell me that they appreciate me sharing my journey about being a single mum, like breaking the stereotype and not being ashamed, and just being proud of who I am . . . everyone makes mistakes, but I want my son to know that I really wanted him and he is very loved. I don't need a husband to provide for my son, I just need to make sure I can still provide for him.

For both of these Influencer mothers, the acrobatic contemplations they made while deciding to debut their babies and pivot their contents appear to be out of necessity: to continue earning an income, to retain their followers, to quell the potential of doxxing, to resist the stereotypes about being young (unwed) mothers, and to integrate their children into the Influencer practices that they have honed over their already-successful careers.

Proximate Micro-celebrification

The term 'microcelebrity' was first used to describe the emerging trend of camgirls who used blogs and videos to share snippets of their everyday lives and cultivate an audience. The concept, which is foundational to the field of Influencer studies, was coined by performance studies scholar Theresa Senft (2008), who studied these young vloggers in the US in the early-2000s. Drawing on the cornerstone scholarship on celebrity studies by sociologist Chris Rojek (2001), communication scholar Alice Marwick subsequently (2013: 116–17) offered that microcelebrity can be 'ascribed' when the person becomes recognizable and legible through user-produced online memes and exposure, or 'achieved' when they themselves engage in strategies of self-presentation like parasociality, intimate exchange and selective disclosure. Micro-microcelebrities are fostered through a process that is in between.

The fame of micro-microcelebrities is first 'achieved' through their continuous exposure to the public by their Influencer mothers, often beginning as ultrasound photographs as foetuses or represented through pregnant bellies. Later on, their celebrity is also 'ascribed' when followers of their Influencer mothers go on to become followers of the child, in turn popularizing public interest and discourse about them through fan chatter, gossip forums, reposts of contents and fan remixes. In other words, the microcelebrity bestowed upon the children of Influencer mothers is entirely contingent upon their proximity to the Influencer and her fame to begin with. Indeed, there were many instances where some of the aspirational or lower-tier Influencers I have studied across the years attempted to launch their children into social media careers, but because the mothers had never accumulated sufficient microcelebrity to begin with, their 'launches' never warranted audience interest in their (very adorable and beautiful) children. However, for the most successful of micro-microcelebrities, fandom can be extreme.

Baby Fandom

Shortly after the first cohort of micro-microcelebrities were born, the first fan meet-and-greets occurred around the mid-2010s. These were (usually paid or otherwise exclusive) opportunities for fans to meet with Influencer mothers and their micro-microcelebrity children in the flesh. At times, these were sponsored events in tie-ups with various brands where fans could also try out services or sample products promoted by the Influencer. But there are also instances when the event was just a pure photo opportunity.

In the early years of my digital ethnography, I catalogued one example of such an event held to celebrate the first birthday of a micro-microcelebrity. In various fan videos and online posts, long lines of adults were seen in a queue, waiting for their turn to pose with the toddler. The child was seated in a baby highchair, positioned in front of a backdrop featuring a birthday banner and some balloons, with mum right next to them. Video footage from the Influencer mother's own vlog of the event shows a rotating crowd of adult fans joining mother and child on centre stage and posing for a throng of event photographers snapping away. In the early days, comments sections of the vlog were mostly starstruck and celebratory, but in later years, some viewers began to question if the child was a willing participant, and contemplate concerns around privacy and wellbeing.

Figure 2.1. Artist impression of a micro-microcelebrity child's first birthday celebration, attended by fans who are queueing for a photo opportunity and a throng of photographers.

The teen Influencer mother that I had mentioned above also revealed in an interview with a social news outlet that she is sometimes surprised by 'fans' of her son. She explains that they are sometimes spotted in public, and she is always taken aback that fans want to offer 'some sort of gift' to her child. She speculates that some of these fans may have spotted her from a distance, and rushed to purchase a gift – such as the time she was having lunch with her family at a cafe. In other instances, fans dig through their belongings to offer her son little treats like candy. She says that for the most part, it is really nice for her son to be so cherished and loved, but she tries to teach him that these are exceptional moments rather than an implicit expectation. In closing another similar interview with a reporter on video, she quips: 'Sometimes I think I am losing my fans to him!' But when pressed by the interviewer, she reveals on a more serious note that she takes the privacy of her son seriously, and is wary of who may be watching or hovering close by when they are out in public.

Props

Dash (born in 2013), of the channels Clicknetwork and Xiaxue, is from Singapore and has been on YouTube since 2013. He is a second-generation microcelebrity born to a prominent Influencer, Xiaxue, who is among the first generation of Influencers in the country, having started her blog and social media from the mid-2000s. Although Xiaxue originally began as a lifestyle Influencer and helmed her own YouTube series 'Xiaxue's Guide to Life' on the aggregate content channel Clicknetwork, she began to expand into the parenting genre after giving birth to Dash by intensively curating his social media presence from conception.

Dash is usually incorporated into his Influencer mother's mostly sponsored videos. By way of advertising the sponsored message, his mother interacts with him on camera while engaging in an activity using the sponsored product or service. When Dash was younger and needed assistance sitting in a single spot to be filmed, he was seen being coaxed by the disembodied arms of his domestic helper from off-screen, or seemingly being bribed or distracted with food to stay in the frame. When Dash was slightly older, these gestural negotiations were managed by his mother, or he would be strapped into a baby highchair in order to stay in the frame. When he was learning to be verbal, his mother would occasionally further engage him in the content by prompting him to respond to their interactions with the product they are testing on camera (i.e. 'Is this nice?', 'Do you want?'). He would reply meekly but rarely addressed the camera directly. At times, Dash would exclaim words and short phrases (i.e. 'Chocolate!', 'Nice!'), to which his mother would usually swiftly acknowledge him, then attempt to weave this 'intrusion' back into the narrative script for the vlog.

In a video sponsored by printer brand Epson (@Xiaxue 2018), Dash's mother attempts to bridge her promotional spiel

Figure 2.2. Artist impression of a micro-microcelebrity child being held in the frame between his mum's thighs.

with updates on her child's growth milestones, explaining how their recreational activities have changed now that Dash is four-and-a-half-years-old. They engage in handicrafts with paper cutouts printed by the printer featured on screen; then the scene cuts to another clip where the Influencer mother promotes the product in detail. Dash returns later in the video and is seen completing spelling exercise sheets, presumably printed with the sponsored product, with the help of his mother. His mother is seen guiding his hand to retrieve the paper from the printer and, when he fidgets, she places him front and centre of the camera by having him stand between her knees while she sits and 'clenches' him in place with her thighs. Subsequently, Dash is seen going off-camera, pressing his face against the lens in a close-up blurred image, and prancing around the couch behind his mother, uninterested in the activity.

In a second video on Xiaxue's dedicated YouTube series (@clicknetwork 2017), she works through a try-out/tutorial of novelty Japanese miniature home cooking by herself. After the eight-minute mark, she transits to include Dash in her video:

> so now that everything is done, I've got Dash here with me, and to see whether I can trick him into eating it . . . now we're going to see his reaction to the tiny little food.

Dash's mother introduces him to the various foods she has made, asking which one he wants to try. He makes his selection and slowly reaches towards an item, but his arms are repeatedly held back or pushed back by his mother, who also shushes him when he interjects with verbal responses. Instead, Dash's mother quizzes him on the names of the foods, and only after he correctly guesses them for the camera is he rewarded with the items he has selected. During the outro, Dash is noticeably uninterested in filming as he leans away from his mother, nears the edge of the frame, appears visibly restless, looks out of frame, and fidgets around. However, he is unable to extract himself this time as he is sat in a baby highchair. As his mother gives her closing words, she wraps her arms around Dash, brings him into the centre of the frame and closer to her, then waves her audience goodbye while Dash's eyes are still focused off-screen.

Across the videos featuring Dash on both channels, he is often seen being enticed by rewards for compliance to stay in the frame and to continue filming. In some videos he is front and centre of the screen but not engaged with the filming despite his mother's cajoling, choosing instead to fixate on his own activities. Dash very rarely makes eye contact with the camera or acknowledges it, perhaps because of his young age, but appears to be thrust in front of it nonetheless. In general, the parental involvement in Dash's videos is extremely high, especially in front of the camera, where he is positioned to be in specific postures and prompted to respond in specific ways (verbally, gesturally, etc.). As many of these videos are sponsored collaborations, Dash's appearances are often used to promote content even though it is not clear to audiences if he is formally or contractually engaged in the filming of the product. At the time of writing, Dash is ten-years-old and no longer appears in his mum's vlogs as she has pivoted to video podcasting on YouTube.

Debuting Digital Estates

As micro-microcelebrity culture became more mainstream and the practice more accepted, subsequent Influencer mothers were more deliberate when introducing their children-to-be to the public. By the mid-2010s, it was commonplace to see carefully designed pregnancy announcements, at times even in partnership brands promoting pregnancy test kits, prenatal vitamins, maternity wards in hospitals and private ob/gyns. But unlike the earlier announcements that simply featured a sonogram or a bump, later Influencer mothers used the opportunity to debut new social media handles for their foetuses that were already uniformly established across various platforms. Fans who did not want to follow the new accounts of these babies also had the option of tracking related contents on dedicated hashtags launched by the Influencer mothers. And as this practice became more common in an industry that was growing more saturated by the day, names were of paramount importance.

In one of the group dinners I attended as a plus one of an Influencer manager, I listened in as a group of Influencers brainstormed baby names for one member who was an expectant mother. Among her criteria was wanting the name to begin with a specific letter of the alphabet, wanting the name to 'sound nice' when paired with her husband's last name, and wanting the name to be 'unique'. By 'unique', she did not mean a name that is merely special, but in its most literal sense she wanted a name that was the only one of its kind. This would ensure that her baby's hashtag would be exclusive to her on Instagram and more easily searchable. In the ten years since

Figure 2.3. Artist impression of an Influencer debuting her micro-microcelebrity baby through sonogram pictures and birth announcements on their Instagram account.

I began noting these conversations with Influencer mothers, we see a rising trend of micro-microcelebrity children being assigned middle names, deliberately misspelt iterations of common names, or completely made-up names altogether. In the internet vernacular, these names are collectively known as 'tragedeigh' and a dedicated subreddit and Facebook group to discuss (or mock) such examples boast over 520,000 and over 153,000 members, respectively, at the time of writing.

More importantly, debuting new social media accounts for micro-microcelebrities is strategic for expanding their digital estates, as this gives clients more avenues and literally more 'surfaces' to place their ads. Influencer mothers may charge their standard rate for an Instagram post comprising a tag and a mention in the captions, and charge a subsidized

Figure 2.4. Artist impression of an Influencer documenting her micro-microcelebrity child's milestones on her own Instagram account, and simultaneously posting a different framing of the same contents on the baby's dedicated Instagram account with sponsored brands tagged.

rate on their child's newly launched account for a Reel and a Story. Multiplying the platforms on which they are active, and the number of accounts hosted on each platform, allows Influencer mothers and their micro-microcelebrity children to multiply their revenue streams. But the early separation of micro-microcelebrities from their mothers' accounts also serves to groom a distinct identity for them, allowing the child to emerge as an independent, recognizable persona online. To this end, it is not uncommon for Influencer mothers to curate individual hashtags and social media accounts unique to each child.

Conclusion

The utility of micro-microcelebrities to enhance brand partnerships, increase revenue streams and foster loyalty is only sustained when there is continued coherence between the branding message, its age-appropriateness and the age of the child. My digital ethnography has surfaced examples of an Influencer mother who featured her kindergarten-aged daughters 'playing' with tampons in a photograph, only to attempt a displaced narrative that segues to educating her underage daughters about feminine hygiene. In another example, an Influencer used her three-year-old niece to advertise a fast-food chain, depicting the child about to bite into a burger. In both instances, some followers found the scene 'adorable', 'endearing' and 'cute'; but there was also noticeable pushback from followers who called the parents out for exploiting the image of their child for revenue.

In my corpus of digital ethnographic data is a podcast by a former Influencer mother. In it, she mentions that when her children started attending 'school', she decided to 'take them off' social media altogether, no longer revealing their faces online. She shares her preemptive concerns about the parents of her children's classmates possibly recognizing them, thus jeopardizing their safety and privacy. Like many Influencers, she maintains private and locked social media accounts. Her journey as a regular mother parenting her children continues to be documented there, but only for an audience of trusted friends among whom she finds comfort and support. For some other Influencer mothers, the micro-microcelebrity journeys of their children continue and the children begin to feature as a regular staple in their contents. In many instances, husbands, fathers, partners and other caregivers are also in the picture. For these Influencer parents, the 'family Influencer' genre is big business.

3

Family Influencers

Introduction

In one of the early analysis of vlogs, communication scholars Maggie Griffith and Zizi Papacharissi (2010) comment that a 'wedding and birthday of a child are intimate moments, often reserved for close friends and family', indicating surprise that a vlogger they were studying had shared these moments online. But the turn of the decade saw the rapid rise of family Influencers for whom weddings and birthdays were mere run-of-the-mill staples in their content streams. Public fascination with the inner workings of families dates back to the era of reality TV. I note in prior work (Abidin 2017a) that the popularity of reality TV families is attributed to the audience's interest in 'ordinary celebrities' (Turner 2010: 2) in Hollywood industry otherwise populated by mainstream entertainment celebrities. These reality TV families primarily capture audiences because they are perceived to be spectacles – somewhat ordinary like you and I, yet different enough in specific ways for us to take interest and want to know more. The three main attributes of their spectacularity include being (Abidin 2017a: 3–4):

Extraordinary: Accomplishing remarkable feats, accumulating outstanding achievements, overcoming extreme adversity.
Exotic: Deviating from the norm and usual expectations of typical families, appearing foreign and distant from mainstream society.
Eccentric: Being unconventional, outlandish, aberrant, or abhorrent through controversy or scandal.

However, owing to the mainstream media tropes that increasingly dramatize such reality TV families, there was a market for actual, everyday, ordinary families who would showcase life without the manipulation of corporate producers. This market was where family Influencers on social media, particularly YouTube, fit right in. In short, family Influencers are typically a household unit who come together to vlog about the domesticity, the experience of living together, and progressing through life stages and significant milestones together, specifically for the purposes of establishing themselves enough to monetize their contents. Communication and media scholar Ümit Kennedy (2024) argues that via vlogging family Influencers can construct 'an identity-forming record of family life, and a commercially viable consumable product'. Because the genre accommodates several people in a unit, family Influencers are able to brand themselves in a myriad of ways, and rely on each family member to venture into related genres or produce offshoot contents that grow the diversity of their target demographic (see 'Jebbey Family' below). As such, family Influencers are an instance of 'social media entertainment' (Cunningham and Craig 2019) where the values, structures and practices of the traditional entertainment industry in Hollywood and the emergent strategies and affordances of social media in Silicon Valley may intersect.

Academic research on family Influencers can be arduous to consolidate, in part because there are very many closely related predecessor and successor descriptions for the genre: mummy bloggers, dad vloggers, parent Influencers and the like. Indeed, even some of the most recent scholarship continues to grapple with the vague delineation of these concepts, pointing to how 'kidfluencers' are usually children with their own social media accounts, but that children also feature heavily in parent Influencer contents and appear there to be kidfluencers (e.g. Hudders and Beuckels 2024). But as I remark in earlier chapters, where mummy/parent bloggers historically focused on the experience of parenting per se (see chapter 1), and micro-microcelebrity generally focuses on how Influencer mothers/parents usher their very young children to share in the limelight (see chapter 2), the business of family Influencers usually sees the more-or-less equal participation of partners/parents and their children.

In other words, in the discourse of the content and the branding of their persona, family Influencers aim to present themselves as a coherent unit, a band, a collective pack, rather than a loose aggregate of discrete individuals; consequently, the parasocial and affective ties they aim to foster among followers will rely heavily on family dynamics between the couple/parents, between the parent and child and between child siblings. Ultimately, these decisions about the minutiae of their self-presentation and content production are fundamentally guided by commercial motives. Communication scholars Arantxa Vizcaíno-Verdú and colleagues (Vizcaíno-Verdú et al. 2022) have referred to this dynamic as a 'promotional-private performativity'. This chapter offers insight into the strategies of family Influencers, including their cultivation of 'anchor' and 'filler' contents, how they deploy 'calibrated amateurism' to justify young labour, and how multi-channel network families put their eggs (i.e. child talents) across several baskets (i.e. channels). It closes with a reflection on whether family Influencing is simply an expression of household and familial domesticity, or whether there are more sinister exploitative intentions at play.

'Anchor/Filler' and Changing Contexts

In one of my earlier pieces of work investigating family Influencers, I offer that my longitudinal digital ethnography has identified the rising practice of the genre being constituted of both 'anchor' and 'filler' material (Abidin 2017a: 4). This was especially the case among American family Influencers that proliferated between the early- and mid-2010s, who often established themselves through specific types of performances like comedy skits, singing and instrumental covers, or tutorials of various kinds ranging from craft to home maintenance. 'Anchor material' is the primary content for which these Influencers are known, and appear to be produced with more care and effort, utilizing higher end equipment such as moving image recorders, audio mixers, lighting and props. 'Filler material' is the secondary content for which these Influencers are known and complement the mainstay of their output by giving followers a highly contextualized snapshot of their everyday lives.

Los Angeles-based Canadian family Influencers Eh Bee Family are a unit of four comprising father 'Papa Bee', mother 'Mama Bee', son 'Mr. Bee' and daughter 'Gabriela Bee'. Their family Influencer brand is focused on making 'Family Friendly Videos and Games' (@ehbeefamily 2024a); their content is 'mainly for families' and their goal is to 'inspire and have more fun together' (@ehbeefamily 2024b). Although now primarily focused on YouTube and Instagram, the family first sprung into life on Vine through their series of New Year's Eve celebration videos beginning in 2014 (Eh Bee 2014). Annual renditions of their classic Vine (e.g. Eh Bee 2015) were an anticipated favourite among internet users. On YouTube, the

Figure 3.1. Artist impression of the family influencers Eh Bee Family who first established their popularity on Vine, and who then 'reacted' to their own vines in a typical Q&A video on YouTube.

family was primarily known for their anchor of comedic skits, especially their very popular remixes of hip-hop songs with child-friendly lyrics known as 'KidzBop' (@ehbeefamily 2014). However, they would also occasionally publish filler content that allowed them to break character and address their viewers directly, through behind-the-scenes reels at official events (@ehbeefamily 2016a) or Q&A sessions (@ehbeefamily 2016b). It is in the spaces of this filler content that fans would often assess the parasocial work by the Eh Bee Family, and reveal appreciation for their authenticity maintenance efforts. Typical comments across such videos include sentiments like 'Mama

Table 3.1. Dichotomy of 'anchor' and 'filler' material by family Influencers focused on 'performance' contents, popular in the early to mid-2010s. Table by author.

	Anchor material	**Filler material**
Priority	Primary content	Secondary content
Context	Front stage, centre stage	Back stage, behind-the-scenes
Production	Polished, staged	Spontaneous, raw
Scheduling	Regular	Ad hoc
Function	Entertainment	Authenticity maintenance
Examples	Skits, music covers, tutorials	Q&A, 'reacts', errands

Bee is actually *so nice* despite her character [in the comedic skits, where she is usually the disciplinarian of the household]'; 'really nice to see big brother [son 'Mr. Bee'] show more of his personality in this Q&A'. At the time of writing, they have 10.4 million subscribers and 1,100 videos on YouTube, and over 1.9 million followers and 2,100 posts on Instagram.

In the context of the mid-2010s, family Influencers like the Eh Bee Family used to publish discrete 'anchor' and 'filler' contents, or append 'fillers' to the end of their main videos (Abidin 2017a). However, by the late-2010s, the genre of family Influencers had proliferated, diversified and professionalized so quickly that the mastery of 'anchor' and 'filler' contents was not so neatly categorized. A few patterns were beginning to establish:

Channel focus: Family Influencers who focused entirely on lifestyle vlogging were very quickly dominating the scene, and many new and old channels pivoted away from performances per se especially as the latter took more effort to script and rehearse. In doing so, these videos fulfilled both entertainment and authenticity maintenance functions at once.

Content types: Newer forms were fast becoming popular, including video podcasting and the 'reacts' genre, which many family Influencers became known for as their anchor or primary content. Consequently, the categories of 'anchor' and 'filler' were beginning to meld together.

Scheduling and Context: To multiply their digital estates and expand monetization opportunities (see below), many family Influencers structured their contents around seasons with planned episodes through playlists, or would launch secondary channels to house different contents. As a result, scheduling became more regular for both 'anchor' and 'filler' material, and both had their time in the limelight cultivated by audience anticipation and expectation.

Production value: Technology became more affordable and user-friendly, and the quality of production also rose rapidly. Hence, even back stage or behind-the-scenes contents began to demonstrate professional and polished aesthetics, and it was increasingly difficult to glimpse instances of the less staged, more raw and more relatable supplementary 'B-roll'.

Platform affordances: The introduction and mass uptake of new YouTube features like Shorts and Community provided family Influencers with more social media-like features to communicate parasociality and authenticity maintenance with followers, such that 'filler' material no longer needed to be scheduled into the main roster in the Video tab. In fact, these new features only heightened the distinction between front and back stage as 'Community' members were perceived and narrated in YouTube's branding to be the more interactive and engaging subset of 'Subscribers', for whom additional features could be unlocked.

Nevertheless, the content types previously established as 'filler' material had enduring value, and continued to serve their authenticity maintenance purposes, even if they were no longer as neatly compartmentalized from the main reel. While there are many content types that offer audiences a more intimate glimpse into the intimate lives of family Influencers, the most popular materials tended to include (Abidin 2017a: 4):

Developmental milestones that document the progress young children in the family have made, such as using the potty for the first time or losing their first tooth.

Family occasions that show the family celebrating cultural and religious holidays such as the Fourth of July or Easter and personal commemorations such as birthdays and wedding anniversaries.

Errands that provide snapshots into how family life is managed, such as talking to a mounted camera during meal times or in the car during school runs on-the-go, and appear more haphazard and spontaneous.

Confessions that record the family having a private conversation or sharing personal reflections, such as when parents reveal parenting mistakes or when children reflect on their growing fame.

Reactions that usually catalogue the children's response to current happenings, such as viral videos and global tragedy, to spontaneous questions from parents resulting in nuggets of 'kid wisdom', or to hidden camera setups in which parents prank their children or capture their unexpected acts of kindness in public.

Logistics that broadcast how family Influencers manage the backend of their fame and engagement with followers, such as acknowledging fan mail on camera, holding Question & Answer (Q&A) sessions, hosting Ask Me Anything (AMA) sessions, and archiving behind-the-scenes (BTS) footage at formal client or sponsored events where the family is guest appearing.

Calibrated Amateurism and Justifying Young Labour

The content types mentioned above were aimed at fostering feelings of authenticity, and were also important in that their aesthetic and production quality gave the impression that these interactions were spontaneous, intimate, sincere. 'Calibrated amateurism' is a practice and aesthetic that Influencers adopt to give the impression that they are amateurs, regardless of their actual content production and professionalism, in order to maintain the veneer of being mere demotic everyday people who feel more authentic and relatable to viewers, despite their status or power in the industry (Abidin 2017a). In other words, they labour over performances of contrived authenticity that are carefully orchestrated (see Goffman 1956) and artfully staged (e.g. MacCannell 1973). Influencers achieve calibrated amateurism through the use of platform affordances and features, and their knowledge of technical tools and cultural vernacular. In other words, they produce the 'raw aesthetic of an amateur, whether or not they really are amateurs by status or practice' (Abidin 2017a: 1).

A family Influencer unit that does this well is the Reality Changers, a Hispanic family based in California initially comprising single dad Jorge and his two daughters, Alexa and Eliana. In later years, the girls' mother and their little brother also joined their channel, until the parents separated for a second time. The Reality Changers first sprang into the spotlight for their song cover videos on YouTube. In particular, their rendition of 'Home' by Edward Sharpe and The Magnetic Zeros propelled Jorge and older daughter Alexa into instant virality (@realitychangers 2010), and they became renowned as the family of cover performances. Younger daughter Eliana was introduced shortly after through filler contents, showcasing a day in the life of single dad Jorge. Some of Eliana's filler contents ended up attaining virality themselves, in part due to her proximate micro-celebrification (see chapter 2)

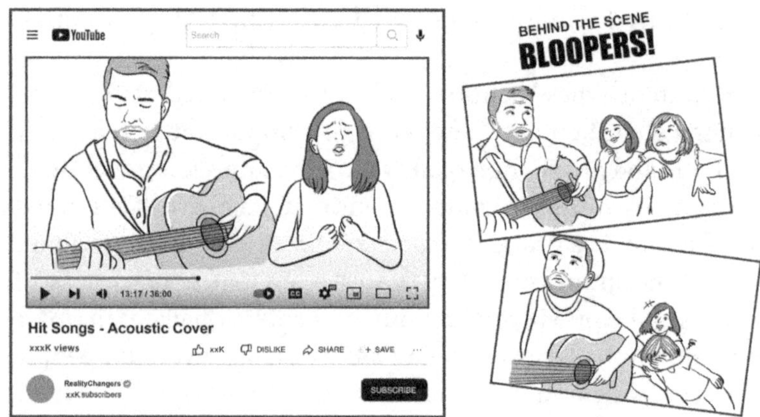

Figure 3.2. Artist impression of the family influencers Reality Changers who first established their popularity on Vine, especially through professional song covers that often included chaotic blooper reels at the end.

for being viral sensation Alexa's sister, and in part because of her humorous childlike quips and antics. These include Eliana encountering death for the first time when her goldfish had died, and she pleaded with her pet to 'wake up' from 'taking a nap' (@realitychangers 2011a), and when asked by Jorge if she likes 'boys or girls', she responds 'I don't like boys! I like Netflix. . . and birds!' (@realitychangers 2011b).

More crucially, these off-stage 'filler' contents were avenues that allowed viewers to have a glimpse of Alexa and Eliana's apparent agency, wherein their actions and quips are interpreted as proxies for active consent in their participation of family Influencer videos (see also chapter 10). I previously reviewed (Abidin 2017a: 11–12) several instances where Reality Changers use their B-roll to demonstrate how, despite having to rehearse for their music cover performances, father Jorge generally allows his daughters to exercise creativity in contributing to the content, and freedom in choosing how active they would like to be. These include moments where Jorge's talking head vlogs to his followers are interrupted by his daughters trying to playfully obstruct the camera lens, and he responds by truncating his address and reciprocating in play rather than disciplining his daughters (@realitychangers 2014a). In another video where he is recounting the family's attendance at VicCon (@realitychangers 2014b), he pans the camera to Alexa to interrupt her gameplay on the family desktop and ask what her favourite part of the event was. She gives a disinterested answer before trailing off to refocus on her game, and Jorge swiftly pivots the audience address to discuss Alexa's love of Minecraft, allowing her to take their filming 'off-track', so to speak.

Multi-Channel Network Families

Titan Digital Media claims to be 'Singapore's largest media and entertainment powerhouse' with '1000+ returning global partnerships every year' and '100+ million monthly organic views'; it manages '22+ creator channels' with a '10 million subscriber base' (Titan Digital Media 2024). At the helm of the company are veteran Singaporean Influencer JianHao Tan, who has been in the business since 2010, and his wife Debbie. The couple also have a daughter, Starley Tan, who is five-years-old at the time of writing. The trio are collectively known as 'Jebbey Family' online.

The Tans manage a multi-channel network on YouTube, each branded differently to venture into various YouTube genres, to target a diversity of viewer demographics, and to appeal to different verticals of potential advertisers. An example of five of the channels that have included Starley as a talent are:

'JEBBEY FAMILY': The channel that most closely aligns with the family Influencer brand, with 1.66 million subscribers (@jebbey 2024a)

'JianHao Tan': Tan's first channel, boasting 7.71 million subscribers (@jianhao 2024)
'Hao': Tan's secondary channel, boasting over 233,000 followers (@jianhao2 2024)
'LADIES FIRST': Initially helmed by wife Debbie before other women Influencers from the Titan Digital Media talent network began to share the channel, with over 441,000 subscribers (@LADIESFIRSTTVSG 2024)
'TEAM TITAN': The flagship vlogging channel for the entire company, featuring its array of talents, with over 543,000 subscribers (@TEAMTITANOFFICIAL 2024)

The JEBBEY FAMILY channel is the family Influencer channel in the most traditional sense. The channel's header image features Starley flanked by both her parents, and the family blowing bubbles together. Some of the top performing videos focus specifically on special occasions and milestones for Starley, and average 150,000 views. Examples include:

- 'Taking my 5 year old daughter on a day out without my husband' with 104,000 views (@jebbey 2024b)
- 'Our daughter answers questions everyone has been asking' with 183,000 views (@jebbey 2024c)
- 'Surprising our 5-year-old daughter with a Pokémon themed party!' with 165,000 views (@jebbey 2024d)
- 'Surprising my daughter with a mermaid themed room in Hong Kong' with 242,000 views (@jebbey 2024e)

However, Starley's cameos in the other channels invite fans of the family to cross over, be exposed to other content genres, and subsequently expand the overall subscriber base of their collective network. My digital ethnography has catalogued videos across the network that have featured Starley in the video cover image, including:

Baby Starley Essentials
LADIES FIRST
xxxK views • 4 years ago

Baby Starley Guesses What's In The Box?!
JEBBEY FAMILY
xxxK views • 2 years ago

Surprising My Wife with a Birthday Trip to Genting!
JEBBEY FAMILY
xxxK views • 4 months ago

Figure 3.3. Artist impression of the family Influencers Jebbey Family and the scope of their contents across various channels on YouTube.

- 'A day in JianHao's life as a dad (in quarantine)' (@jianhao 2020)
- 'Preparing my 4-year-old daughter's dream birthday' (@jianhao2 2023)
- 'Baby's nursery room tour!' (@LADIESFIRSTTVSG 2019)
- 'JianHao and Debbie's baby is here! – Team Titan Vlogs' (@TEAMTITANOFFICIAL 2019)

The group of Starley videos on the channel JianHao Tan (@jianhao) and Hao (@jianhao2) are a mix of skits and vlogs that feature Starley as the main character or a cameo. However, the narration mostly focuses on Tan's journey as a business owner, Influencer and young father. The group of videos on LADIES FIRST (@LADIESFIRSTTVSG) are narrative through wife/mum Debbie's perspective, and focus on parenting hacks and tips through sponsored product and service recommendations. However, with the exception of the 2019 video announcing the arrival of Starley (@TEAMTITANOFFICIAL 2019), the other videos show Starley as a cameo, and the placement of her image centre stage on the YouTube cover image appears to serve as clickbait.

Expression or Exploitation?

An argument in support of the family Influencer genre is that it allows for a diversity of family units to showcase their everyday lives, lived as forms of intercultural learning. Many family Influencers also argue that their children enjoy the sense of confidence that comes from learning to express themselves well, and receiving affection from viewers in return. Yet, alongside the risks already discussed in the opening of this chapter, there is a rising number of prolific scandals pointing to the family Influencer genre as a hotbed for child exploitation.

American family Influencers DaddyOFive are known for making YouTube videos of the parents pranking their children, even if several of these pranks veer between harmless practical jokes and highly distressing mistreatment for the children. These include 'pranks' of the father filming himself orchestrating a mess in his son's room, then scolding his son for it to the point of tears, only to reveal that it was a setup. In yet another video, the father had ordered his children to repeatedly slap one of their sisters as a 'prank'. In 2017, a band of YouTube viewers reported the parents to child protection services for child abuse, leading to an investigation and YouTube pulling advertising from the channel (Leaver and Abidin 2017). The parents were eventually convicted of child neglect, sentenced to five years' probation, and lost custody of two of their children (Hern 2018). Scholars have long observed

Figure 3.4. Artist impression of a family influencer who is known for being embroiled in several controversies where their children are filmed on video crying or looking visibly annoyed.

how family vlogging in this sense can bring significant distress to the child, especially if they have little to no autonomy or ability to understand the context and provide ongoing consent to be filmed (Chalklen and Anderson 2017).

Because these incidents took place in discrete videos over several months, chatter and call-outs on various online fora (see chapter 10) express continued frustration, concern and eventually fatigue over these supposed 'antics'. But there are other instances where child 'exploitation' is more morally grey, such as when toddlers and teenagers appear distraught or unwilling to be on camera.

Conclusion

I close with reflections on what happens when relationships break down and families separate, and family Influencers feel pressured to housekeep their domestic issues in the public eye. A family Influencer whom I had been studying in my digital ethnography abruptly announced that husband and wife were separating and moving to different countries. Despite their separation having happened several months prior, the couple only made the news public when their divorce proceedings had been finalized. Their YouTube announcement also detailed the logistics of how they were going to co-parent their child and manage their YouTube brand. Many fans in the comments section expressed sympathy for their situation, but still many others criticized the couple for being 'dishonest', 'deceitful' and 'keeping the news' from them. In a follow-up video, the couple calmly responded that they needed time off-camera to organize their personal matters, and only shared the news when they were ready. They also needed to consult business partners, clients and lawyers regarding the splitting of their assets, and to strategize over the continuation of their careers as full-time Influencers. Several months on, mother and child continue to feature on the flagship family Influencer channel as a duo, while father and child now feature in a secondary channel focused on gameplay and tech. The child now lives in two homes across two cities, and two Influencer brands across two channels.

These instances reveal the very strong buy-in that followers feel when they subscribe to family Influencers, and feel like members of a very extended social media family. They underscore the challenges experienced by family Influencers, who feel pressured to offer an accounting of all domestic decisions – no matter how minor or major – to preempt accusations of inauthenticity or lack of transparency. However, for the most part many of the parents in these family Influencer units are able to strategically narrate their executive decision making as legal guardians of the children in their unit, and assume responsibility for any backlash or fallout. For a different category of 'internet famous' children, the vague label of being 'child Influencers' eludes clear responsibilization, as we will observe in the next chapter.

4

Child Influencers

Introduction

As noted in the Introduction, 'Child Influencers' has become the catch-all term for all forms of 'internet famous' children. Yet, the scholarship has yet to consider nuanced delineations of related concepts and theorizations, and distinct origin stories and socio-political contexts. For instance, articles claiming to be overviews of child Influencer research are still caught in a bind of imprecise definitional and scaffolding work; one study surveyed as few as twenty-three articles focusing explicitly on just the phenomenon of 'toy unboxing', despite being titled as a 'research agenda' on child Influencer research (Rotimi et al. 2024). Most of the research on child Influencers and related phenomena has focused overtly on YouTube. These include a specialized focus on specific genres like toy unboxing on YouTube (Craig and Cunningham 2017; Marsh 2016; Martínez and Olsson 2019; Nicoll and Nansen 2018); 'disturbing' contents in children's YouTube genres (Balanzategui 2021); a survey of child-targeted platforms like YouTube Kids (Burroughs 2017); the regulation of advertising by 'kidfluencers' on YouTube specifically (Feller and Burroughs 2021); or more nuanced scholarship on children's literacies and the value of using collaborative social networks like YouTube to negotiate identity (Lange 2014). However, the work of this book and this chapter in particular focuses on conceptual delineations of who gets to be defined as a 'child Influencer' and why this is important.

While on an international scale there is a lack of knowledge and guidance in formulating policy to protect the wellbeing of child Influencers, France and the UK have been leading the charge by first beginning with defined boundaries of what and who constitutes a 'child Influencer'. In a world-first, France passed a law in 2020 to extend regulation from the traditional entertainment industries to cover *children who work in social media* (Kumar 2020, emphasis mine). This applies even to the grey area of *children who produce content not yet deemed as professionals* (Library of Congress 2020, emphasis mine). France has also enacted the General Data Protection Regulation (GDPR) to require social media platforms to remove content of child Influencers upon request (Rieffel 2023). Video producers, including parents, who do not comply face hefty fines and even a jail term (Kumar 2020). In the UK, the Digital, Culture, Media and Sport Committee held hearings with expert witnesses to consider similar regulation for Influencers in the country (UK Parliament 2021, 2022). The 2024 update to the Coogan Law in the US also reflects wording that defines 'child Influencers' as 'influencers and online content creators who are minors' (Kilkenny 2024), including those who appear in contents posted by their Influencer parents.

Thus, the intricate work of defining whether or not an 'internet famous' child falls under the category of a 'child Influencer' is not a matter of pedantics, but results directly in their perception by the public, by industry stakeholders and by the law, which in turn impacts the extent of platform and policy provisions entitled and available to them. In this chapter, we consider how some parents (strategically) enact ambiguity and plausible deniability in deflecting suggestions that their 'internet famous' child is a 'child Influencer', in a bid to reduce their responsibilization discourse under which they are pressured to act. We then consider three case studies of loosely-defined 'child Influencers' in three socio-cultural contexts to underscore the importance of locating the 'techno-literacy practices' (Marsh 2004) of children online, to assess the potentials and pitfalls of their internet celebrity in context, rather than throw the baby out with the bathwater. For Thailand-based Deksorkrao, their advantageous brokerage of visibility has led to opportunities for economic mobility; for China-based Niuniu, the lack of clarity regarding her status between the modelling and social media industries has seen behind-the-scenes abuse go unregulated for a period of time; and for US-based Ryan, the tried-and-tested modalities of his child YouTuber unboxing strategies have meant that he continues to play the 'eternal child' after more than a decade and even as he grows into teenhood.

Ambiguity and Plausible Deniability

In this section, we consider three brief, pseudonymous case studies from my ethnographic fieldwork, discussing how some parents of 'internet famous' children negotiate whether or not their ward is an Influencer, regardless of the extent and nature of their visibility online.

Just a 'plus-one'

Sienna considers herself a 'lifestyle Influencer' and her contents cover a wide variety of genres including beauty, fashion, health and fitness, parenting and even sex advice. In the years when her son was a toddler then a kindergartener, followers began to notice that Sienna often brought her child along to brand events. The evidence is in years of Instagram posts and

YouTube videos, as well as follower reports widely discussed on Influencer forums (see chapter 10). Followers often questioned if Sienna's son was attending kindergarten or if he had alternative care arrangements, and called her out for 'dragging' her son along to work. While one segment of her followers insisted that she issue a public apology, or be held responsible by authorities overseeing child welfare, another segment began to suggest that Sienna's son was effectively working as a 'child Influencer', as he featured so prominently throughout her contents. Further, a large portion of Sienna's followers were fans mainly because of her son.

When she finally issued a response, Sienna insisted that her son was 'not personally involved' in any of her clients' events, and was merely 'taken along' with her to stay by her side. When he features in her contents filmed at home, she argues, the setup is similar to a 'work from home' arrangement that any parent might be familiar with, so it is 'natural' that her son is present. Sienna asserts that her son is not 'used' in any 'advertising', but is included in her personal narration of the product or service because he is 'so much a part of [her] life'. However, followers remained unconvinced, and amassed evidence of Sienna using her son as 'cute bait' to capture and maintain follower interest in her sponsored social media posts. The discussion came to a standstill, the allegations of child exploitation still continue, and Sienna maintains that her son is just her 'plus-one' at work events and in everyday life.

Not 'sponsored' but still 'monetized'

Melanie is a veteran Influencer who often features her children in vlogs recounting her routine as a working mother. Some years ago, one of Melanie's vlogs attracted viral attention on an international scale when she was seen pranking her children (see also chapter 3). For a week, she was chastised in a variety of languages and resorted to locking some social media accounts for a few days. When the furore had faded, Melanie clarified that her children were willing participants in the prank, and that they had collectively planned the 'script' and 'staged' the scenario for laughs. She asserts that her children enjoyed the activity, which she perceived to be the opportunity for them to 'experience and understand a little more about her life as a content creator'. In closing her statement, Melanie adds that she was 'just a regular mum', and that more importantly, her children were 'not child Influencers' but just 'regular kids'. She maintains that she would 'never use them for sponsored content' unless she was featuring child-related brands for clients.

However, after her statement the furore was reignited. In various forums and YouTube hate vlogs, followers called Melanie out for insisting that her children were never used for 'sponsored content' as, in their view, the viral traffic she received on her vlog was specifically because of her children 'acting' in the 'prank'; further, as a participant in the platform's creator rewards programme, she had ultimately monetized the viral video. In other words, followers insisted that while Melanie's children did not feature in 'sponsored content', they were still used to 'monetize content'. Even though Melanie did not respond any further and interest in the 'scandal' soon died down, the minutiae of distinctions remain an interesting discussion in Influencer hate blogs and forums today.

Photography 'in situ' vs in 'professional settings'

Gabby started out as a popular fashion blogger in her twenties, but eventually moved to run an online fashion brand in her thirties. On her online store, the wares were modelled by professional adult and child models, usually shot in photo studios. Little is known about these models as they were working professionals in the modelling industry and hired through an agency; in other words, the models were strictly not Influencers. Like most brands, the photographs used on her online store were also cross-posted on the brand's social media accounts for publicity. However, Gabby also had the practice of dressing herself and her daughter in the clothes she was selling whenever they went on outings. She would snap photographs of mother and child, at times while posing at landmarks or scenic sights, and at times more casually when they were out and about. A comment from a fan on Instagram suggested that Gabby's daughter, then seven-years-old, was beautiful and should 'become an actual model'. This comment was well received by other followers and 'liked' thousands of times, and was thus automatically ranked as a 'top comment' and spotlighted on Gabby's Instagram post. Gabby's reply to the comment, which was also spotlighted, thanked the fan for the compliment, but said that her daughter 'isn't a model' and 'does not intend to become one'.

Perhaps unexpectedly, hundreds of fans replied to this thread, calling Gabby a 'hypocrite' as she had long been using her daughter to 'model' and 'advertise' children's clothes on her social media. They insisted that Gabby should hire and feature her daughter 'properly' as she would any of the professional models that she casts for her campaign shoots. Although Gabby never responded thereafter, the long stream of comments broke into a debate over when the work constitutes 'child labour', and whether or not Gabby's daughter was 'working' as a model or doing mum a 'favour'. As I closely followed this discussion in my digital ethnography, an interesting distinction that surfaced was whether Gabby's daughter was filmed 'in her natural habitat' [*sic*] or 'in the studio'. In other words, followers were locating the environment of the photographs, citing that because Gabby and her daughter were in situ, and going about their daily routine, Gabby was not actually in a workplace and was not placed under the confines of a professional work setting.

These vignettes demonstrate the need for a framework of clear and precise definitional work to understand the role of children in commercial social media marketplaces, if we were to triage them through different options and streams of governance and regulation, such as through labour laws (e.g. Verdoodt et al. 2020). They allow us to acknowledge the unique positionality of the 'internet famous' children through different iterations, and understand how and why they might be falling through the gaps of advertising and marketing guidelines that do not yet account for their rights or wellbeing.

Advantageous Brokerage of Visibility: Deksorkrao

There are a myriad of risks and dangers to which 'internet famous' children are vulnerable, and these are discussed throughout the book. But in this section, we consider an example when the visibility of 'internet famous' children can be advantageous, through the example of prominent K-pop cover artists Deksorkrao (เด็กเซาะกราว) from Thailand. I note that there is not yet a widely accepted agreement as to 'what' type of 'internet celebrity' the Deksorkrao girls are; in their YouTube videos, they appear to have been featured in a handful of sponsored contents, and their viral K-pop cover videos are monetized on YouTube. Their YouTube bio lists contact information, presumably for clients to reach their manager, but not much else is known about them in the English-language media. While the very few news articles that have profiled them have variously referred to the girls as 'cover artists', 'performers' and 'YouTube stars', Thailand-based talent and Influencer managers whom I have personally interviewed in the course of my fieldwork have referred to Deksorkrao as 'a special type of child Influencer', and as 'unique kid YouTubers'. Paying deference to local market norms and mores, in this section I discuss Deksorkrao as child Influencers.

I first chanced upon Deksorkrao in 2016, via their viral video parodying the official music video of 'Playing With Fire' by the K-pop girl group BLACKPINK (@deksorkrao 2016). In it, four young Thai girls are filmed dancing and acting out BLACKPINK's music video with high precision, and even the camera work, framing and angles were accurate to the original. But what stood out was that while BLACKPINK were filmed in expensive and highly decorated studio sets, the Deksorkrao video was simply set, in a village in Thailand – sandy ground, muddy feet, wooden huts, grassy plains, wild animals roaming, household goods and assorted paraphernalia of country life galore. This would go on to become their trademark, as they parodied the music videos of more BLACKPINK productions, and later of other K-pop idols. At the time of my last data collection in 2023, Deksorkrao had over 2.82 million subscribers on YouTube over a collection of 232 videos. At the time of writing, they now boast over 3.84 million subscribers over 642 videos. They have since expanded to TikTok (3 million followers), Instagram (338,000 followers) and Facebook (1.7 million followers). Their bio lists contact details like an email address, phone number and a LINE handle (@deksorkrao 2024). The videos are produced by one of the girl's older brothers, who also brokers their sponsored opportunities and manages their YouTube channel.

While Deksorkrao has now established themselves as K-pop cover artists more generally, their initial rise to fame focused exclusively on BLACKPINK music videos, of which their channel curates a playlist of hit songs (@deksorkrao 2022). Each Deksorkrao member consistently plays the same BLACKPINK idol: Kungten plays Jennie, Kwang plays Jisoo, Som plays Rosé and Mommaem plays Lisa. Consider the example of Deksorkrao's cover of BLACKPINK's 'As If It's Your Last' (@deksorkrao 2018): where BLACKPINK are stylized in high school uniforms and dancing on a stage that resembles the Colosseum in Rome, Deksorkrao are dressed in their actual school uniforms and dancing in a village with a tiled roof house and wooden hut in the background. In a scene where

YouTube

Reaction Video! BLACKPINK x DEKSORKRAO – 'Lovesick Girls' M/V

Figure 4.1. Artist impression of girl group Deksorkrao, who became popular on YouTube for their performance of BLACKPINK cover music videos, reacting to composites of their cover videos played alongside the BLACKPINK originals.

BLACKPINK's Rosé is sitting inside an expensive convertible and turns to face the camera at the back, Deksorkrao's Som is sitting in an old pushcart while emulating the same gestures and captured with the same camera angle.

What started out as mere fun slowly became a hobby through the first wave of parody cover videos, and eventually culminated in more polished and creative parody covers that invited sponsorship and more paid advertising opportunities in partnership with tech brands and events organizers. For child Influencers like Kungten, Kwang, Som and Mommaem, the visibility of internet celebrity can be mediated to be advantageous with tangible consequences for social-economic mobility. These case studies remind us to adopt a more localized and nuanced approach in our consideration of child Influencers, as the morality of childhood fame is differently interpreted, received, negotiated and challenged in different socio-cultural and socio-economic contexts, and ultimately contingent upon local mores, norms, values and economic opportunity.

Behind-the-Scenes Abuse: Niuniu

> [R]elying on your child to earn money is one thing but yet you still kick her?
> I really feel for your daughter. At that age she's supposed to be carefree, but she's making money for you. She is not a tool.

Above is a selection of damning comments against the mother of Niuniu, a three-year-old child model based in Hangzhou, China, who went viral internationally after a video of her mother kicking her surfaced and was viewed over 22 million times by viewers on Chinese and international platforms (Bramwell and Allen 2019). News reports assert that Niuniu had been modelling for just over half a year (Ni 2019), but she was already widely known as a 'social media child star' (Yahoo News Australia 2019) owing to being 'a well-known clothes model' (Bramwell and Allen 2019). Niuniu was allegedly being punished by her mother while in the midst of modelling clothes for an online store, for which the parent faced a 'wave of criticism online in China' and was denounced for her 'suspected domestic violence' (Bramwell and Allen 2019).

Shortly after, another video surfaced showing Niuniu's mother shouting at her in a dressing room and using a clothes hanger to hit her (Huang 2019). The public discourse on child models like Niuniu began to include persistent issues like young children working long hours (e.g. 0900–0200hrs),

Figure 4.2. Artist impression of popular child model Niuniu, who went viral when blurry behind-the-scenes images allegedly exposed her parents abusing her.

missing school, and even modelling for bikinis at car shows. News reports and users pointed to instances of other parents seen harshly disciplining their children behind-the-scenes of photoshoots (Huang 2019). News reports also revealed that while earlier iterations of child labour laws in China prohibit children under the age of sixteen from working as 'full-time employees' (Li 2019), these laws are not yet extended to consider the ad hoc work conducted by child models like Niuniu, who are usually hired by the hour or by the day. It was also noted that current advertising laws prohibit companies from 'using minors under the age of 10 as spokespeople' (Yahoo News Australia 2019). The collective public outcry led to 'over 100 kidswear shops' on e-commerce website Taobao issuing 'a joint statement calling for regulation and oversight of the country's child modelling industry' (Ni 2019). Among the terms, the shops voluntarily pledged to (Ni 2019):

- standardize procedures for photoshoots involving children;
- forbid all forms of violence against children; and
- refuse to use photos or videos if the children would be at risk of being harmed.

A month later, in May 2019, new regulations were issued by the prosecutor in Hangzhou (Huang 2019) stipulating that:

- Child models under the age of 10 are forbidden from endorsing brands;
- Companies are not allowed to overwork the same child model to the extent that it leads to absences from school;
- Companies are not allowed to have child models work continuously for over four hours;
- Child models cannot be forced to wear unsuitable clothing or perform age-inappropriate acts; and
- Companies must not impose any kind of physical or mental abuse on child models.

The regulations were heralded as the 'first of [their] kind specifically relating to child modeling in China' (Huang 2019). As many child Influencers in the Chinese market often begin their careers as child models (see chapter 9), the extension of these clear and specific guidelines to comprehensively overhaul the governance of children in the child model industry will have positive spillover effects on the child Influencer industry over time.

The 'Eternal Child': Ryan of Ryan's World

Launched in March 2015, with over 38.8 million subscribers, over 59 billion views, and over 3,100 videos at the time of writing, Ryan's World – previously known as Ryan ToysReview – is a YouTube channel fronted by American child Influencer

Ryan Kaji. The channel's description (@RyansWorld 2024) reads:

> Welcome To Ryan's World!!! Ryan loves doing lots of fun things like pretend play, science experiments, music videos, skits, challenges, DIY arts and crafts and more!!! Most of the toys we used to review are being donated to local charity Ryan's Toys & Clothing at Walmart and Target!

Ryan debuted on the channel at the age of three, and swiftly rose to mainstream celebrity for his collection of viral videos. He has dozens of endorsement deals, brand partnerships, licence deals and mechanizing arrangements with brands, and has advertised hundreds of brands in his nine-year career thus far. Like many child Influencers, Ryan and his guardians have been embroiled in a series of scandals, including untransparent advertising, YouTube advertorials targeting children who are too young, and the promotion of age-inappropriate products like unhealthy foods. Many of these incidents have resulted in hefty fines, and even changes to YouTube's platform policy to comply with changing regulations. Yet, despite the setbacks, Ryan continues to be the highest earning child Influencer on YouTube and worldwide, and has amassed many accolades for these achievements.

At the time of writing, Ryan is thirteen-years-old. Those who have followed his career for a long time have pointed out that Ryan is now a teenager who is (still) targeting the toddler-to-kindergartener age bracket. Online sleuths (see chapter 10) point to his facial hair, his deepening voice and even the faint acne on his skin to underscore that Ryan is ageing out of the child Influencer industry, and question whether he remains an appropriate role model for the millions of very young children who flock to his videos everyday – his best performing videos have accumulated more than 1 billion views. In some ways, Ryan presents an exemplary case study for his (parents')

Figure 4.3. Artist impression of Ryan of Ryan's World, who amassed popularity for toy unboxing videos on YouTube as a child, and who continues to make content in the same genre as a teenager.

successful navigation of the child Influencer industry with very lucrative returns. In other ways, Ryan's career points to the depressing reality that despite a decade of followers pointing out the various issues plaguing the channel, calling out his parents for faux pas and missteps, and underscoring their ongoing concern for his wellbeing, Ryan continues to remain active and centre stage in the child Influencer industry. Ryan's twin sisters, Emma and Kate Kaji, debuted on his channel as infants. At the time of writing, the girls are eight-years-old, and active child Influencers on Ryan's World. Followers speculate that the sisters will inherit and front the channel when Ryan eventually transits out of child Influencing, but they also speculate that not much will change for the children whose childhoods must continue to be extended and commodified to sustain a multi-million-dollar franchise.

Conclusion

This chapter has offered original scaffolding for defining and delineating 'child Influencers' from other forms of 'internet famous' children, considered variants and varieties of child Influencers with different origin stories, showcased the plausible deniability deployed by some parent-guardians to skirt around criticism and governance, contemplated instances where visibility can be positively leveraged for child Influencer socio-economic mobility, and spotlighted how regulation in one sector of the child internet celebrity market can have productive impacts on the child Influencer market as a whole. In the next chapter, we focus on how the internet celebrity of some children is more closely entangled with the specific socio-political and techno-moral panics of platforms, through an in-depth look at KidTok.

5

KidTok

Introduction

In my first stint of digital ethnography on TikTok spanning 2019–2020, I introduced the genre of 'KidTok' as the:

> TikTok accounts dedicated to showcasing babies and very young children [that] tend to catalogue a child's every routine, adorable performances like song-singing, emotive reactions like laughter or tantrums, and even play-acting skits, role-playing, and kid conversations. (Abidin 2021: 93)

At that time, I had been studying the phenomenon of child internet celebrity across several social media platforms, but noted that KidTok '[did] not yet seem to receive the same backlash or yield the same moral panics' (Abidin 2021: 93) as did predecessor phenomena like 'sharenting' (Blum-Ross and Livingstone 2017). I offered that this could have been because KidTok content was still generally short (at under one minute at that time) unlike the longform content of family vlogs on YouTube, and that KidTok posts were more casual snippets and did not give much personal information away, unlike the intimate and regular updates of 'babygram' milestones on Instagram. But much has changed since then.

TikTok is now a hotbed for agents to discover 'TikTok prodigies' – children known for their singing, dancing, acting and performance talents. This has spurred on many TikTokers to duet and react to the contents of these children in order to boost their visibility and enhance their opportunities to be 'spotted' or 'discovered' by talent scouts. Such savvy practices regarding platform visibility have been studied as a form of 'algorithmic mutual aid', which communication scholars Elena Maris and colleagues argue is 'a practice unfolding in platform economies that demonstrates people's increased recognition of the value of their digital labor, and efforts to reorient platform logics of value, visibility, and compensation to care for one another' (Maris et al. 2024: 4071).

But in the brief years since TikTok first exploded into the limelight with young users, some older children themselves are now ushering in the next generation of KidTok. There are a handful of popular TikTokers who are well known for embracing their role as underaged parents. Many of them became pregnant as minors, under-eighteen, when they were arguably still 'children' in the eyes of the law. Like the micro-microcelebrities discussed earlier (see chapter 2), their babies become recipients of fame by proxy, pointing to the increasingly rapid and short life cycles of TikTok generations.

The mass uptake of TikTok during the pandemic has also led to an inevitable consequence: the over-exposure of the domestic locus of the home. TikTokers who are not as privacy-conscious have been called out for revealing their children's school uniforms in the stacks of laundry, showcasing window views that expose their address, and other forms of accidental forms of 'micro-doxxing' by the self. Given the dual uses of the home as centre stage for KidToks, the platform can be collectively interpreted as a digital 'third place' (Oldenburg 1999) – an alternative venue outside of home and work – where people can convene and converse. Given the fast-changing socio-politics of KidTok, sociologist Alex Turvy and I offer an updated definition of KidTok in new work:

> we view KidTok as a *network* of children on TikTok who rise to prominence through algorithmic visibility and recommendation, a *subculture* that challenges the categories and consequences of fame experienced by 'internet famous' children, and a *phenomenon* that opens a fresh set of issues and concerns that effective governance must address, especially as community policing is a mainstay on the platform. (Turvy and Abidin 2025: 2–3, emphasis in original)

Given the tensions between empowerment and endangerment, a brief consideration of KidTok in context is helpful. This chapter provides insight into the dangers and promises of child-centred and child-produced contents on TikTok, and considers three types of case studies: the 'Maia Knight Twins' controversy offers promising developments on how some parents can commit to content pivots to increase the privacy of their child; the 'Pandemic Babies' trend and 'Four Seasons Baby' meme point to how prolific conspiracy theories are on TikTok and how the cute imagery of young children are lubricants for such participatory conversations; and the '#ImJustAKid' challenge demonstrates some of the more lighthearted communal memory making when TikTokers negotiate the contours of a viral vernacular to underscore more wholesome aspects of child image sharing.

Dangers and Promises

A quick scroll through any newsfeed would regularly surface very concerning contents to which young children on TikTok are exposed: a plethora of dangerous challenges, the sexualization of children, parental neglect, the doxxing of once-upon-a-time private citizens, the rapid institution of children as TikTok stars overnight. Academic scholarship on KidTok is often discouraging, with various studies from the health sciences and psychology pointing to TikTok's negative impact on the mental health and wellbeing of children. Studies from the social sciences and humanities usually present a more nuanced verdict.

Hypersexualized contents on TikTok may present opportunity for self-empowerment but the objectification of young bodies can also be akin to bullying (Soriano-Ayala et al. 2023); parents have rightful concerns regarding the privacy of their children on TikTok, but children themselves exhibit uncanny capabilities to 'negotiate boundaries between the public and private' (De Leyn et al. 2022) and do consider safety and wellbeing (Sarwatay et al. 2023). Despite the risks of TikTok use, we also need to consider and preserve the perspectives of children themselves who experience 'joy, connection, and creativity' on the platform (Rodriguez and Zhao 2024: 1). The fictional scenarios roleplayed by mother and father figure characters – known as 'internet parents' – on TikTok can vicariously offer acceptance and affirmation to children, especially those who have felt neglect by their birth parents due to their personal identities (like coming out as queer, or turning away from a religion) or their family circumstances (like children of divorce) (Smith and Mendelson 2024).

Various studies have also observed that despite the risks, older children on TikTok have come together on the platform to pursue different forms of advocacy. My own body of work with various collaborators has studied, for instance, how Black (American) girls on TikTok cultivate a sense of community to share self-care advice that is otherwise suppressed by beauty content predominantly created for White women (Taylor and Abidin 2024); or how young Filipino Gen Zs participate in trolling behaviours like TikTok 'dogshows', but also use the opportunity to learn about the acceptable boundaries of permissible humour and online (in)civility (Cabbuag and Abidin 2024). Yet, politics can go both ways, and TikTok cultures have also been used by radicals to spread far-right ideologies and online racism to young children (Ozduzen et al. 2023).

Gen Z TikTokers from around the world have rehearsed their political consciousness and communication skills by participating in global TikTok trends like '#OkBoomer', where memes are used to express intergenerational politics and identity formation (Zeng and Abidin 2021). During the COVID-19 pandemic, children in primary and high schools were also spending prolonged periods on TikTok to interact with their teachers, who used creative methods to impart important values and keep students engaged despite the challenges of digitized education (Vizcaíno-Verdú and Abidin 2023).

It is under this climate of the pandemic that the focus pivots to the very young children of KidTok: those whose parents offer accounts on their behalf; those who are not yet old enough to offer accounts of agency and joy as above; those whose early childhoods are documented, discoursed and dissected by a collective millions of users worldwide without their knowledge.

'Maia Knight Twins' and Privacy Pivots

Maia Knight is the young mother of twin girls Scout and Violet. The trio rose to fame in the first year of the twins' lives when Knight took to documenting their everyday lives on TikTok in several posts each day. In the early days, she was known for her ability to carry both babies in her arms while completing mundane chores around the house, with her camera capturing the scenes and the intricate facial expressions of both twins. Followers showered the family with affection, celebrated the strength of the single mum, and checked in regularly, citing TikToks of the twins as the highlight of their day.

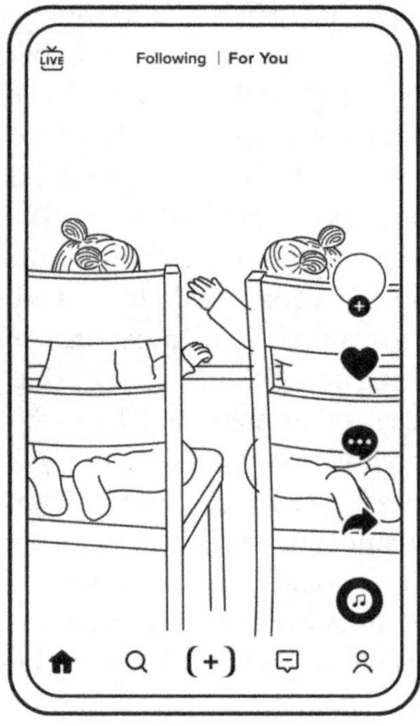

Figure 5.1. Artist impression of TikToker Maya Knight's twins on TikTok, following her decision to conceal their faces in subsequent TikTok posts.

Like predecessor mummy bloggers (see chapter 1) and family Influencers (see chapter 3), Knight's engagement with paid content and other monetized opportunities was met with mixed responses, with some followers applauding her savvy for providing for her family and others accusing her of exploiting her children. In prior work, Turvy and I have discussed this incident at length in prior work reviewing community norms on KidTok (Turvy and Abidin 2025). But here, I focus on what unfolded when Knight turned to concealing her daughters' faces shortly after they turned a year old.

While the 'Maia Knight Twins' were once on full display for the camera – in sufficient detail for watchful audiences to point out boogers and milk residue on their chins in comments sections – Knight began to show the toddlers on camera only if their faces were concealed. In one post, they were seated such that the back of the chair was obscuring their faces. In another post, there were emojis superimposed over their faces. In yet another post, Knight cradled one toddler in one arm while covering her face with the other hand. While followers initially joked about the 'suspense' that Knight was building, a month in, things turned nasty.

Anger and hate flooded the comments sections of the posts, with fans accusing Knight of 'withholding' the twins from them, and that they were entitled to see them as these were the very fans whose daily views and loyalty contributed to their TikTok fame in the first place. Later on, in some talking head commentary in further TikTok posts, Knight explained that as her daughters were maturing into 'recognizable' faces and bodies, she would no longer be showing their faces. Knight's efforts were eventually applauded by followers, among whom some speculated that it was their call-outs of child exploitation that initiated her decision. This form of 'community governance' will be discussed in further detail in chapter 10. Where follower discourse can prove to be productive in some instances, in other instances its utility is more lukewarm or even harmful.

'Pandemic Babies', 'Four Seasons Baby' and Conspiracy Theories

I note in *Australian Quarterly* (Abidin 2023) that against the backdrop of prolonged self-isolation around the world during COVID-19, parents were spending unprecedented periods of time with their young children at home. During this season, many viral TikTok trends focused on young children and their quirks. Parents on a massive scale documented their babies' milestones with excruciating detail. This was in part an act of communion and solidarity with others around the world who

Figure 5.2. Artist impression of one of the common posts from the 'pandemic babies' trend on TikTok, featuring babies achieving amazing feats like crawling or standing well before they arrive at the appropriate age for these milestones.

were struggling with parenting and work-from-home duties, and in part the trend of 'pandemic babies'.

'Pandemic babies' is a popular group of audio memes (see chapter 6 on memes and audio memes) that register the daily lives and milestones of the thousands of babies born during the lockdown. It functions also as an 'inside joke' that babies born during this time were exceptional, as they appeared to be hitting their milestones at a rapid pace.

At first, hundreds of thousands of comments across the repertoire of KidTok videos were debating where the vaccines administered to pregnant women had resulted in 'mutant babies', 'super children' and 'exceptional antibodies' in this cohort of babies. Some parents were also comparing the home video snippets of their 'pandemic babies' with their older children, citing notable distinctions like the ability to independently hold up their heads earlier than usual, strong muscle tone in their thighs leading to standing or walking ahead of their projected growth milestones, or creative interpretations of assorted baby noises as evidence that 'my pandemic baby talks'. It was often difficult to ascertain if these were merely jokes or actual conspiracy theories as TikTokers often deployed humour in deprecating ways, and when specific KidToks become exceptionally viral, people from all walks of life would chime in with their own take. But then compilations of these 'pandemic babies' began to proliferate on the darker side of the web, on online forums dedicated to anti-vaccine proponents, far-right ideologists who refused medical treatment, and even medical forums that were previously used for serious conversation. The lines between joke and conspiracy theory blurred very quickly.

In all likelihood, these propositions can be explained by the increase in time spent both nurturing and documenting the child. Conspiracy theories aside, it was during this time that conversations around the privacy and rights of the child were heightened on TikTok, as all at once at a massive scale globally, babies on the platform were turned into memes, 'befriending' each other in collaborations, and even having their likeness used in compromising 'role-play' content. TikTokers began calling out viral trends, challenges and hashtags that were centred on children, and invited parents to reconsider their practices. A few years into the post-pandemic recovery, conspiracy theories and armchair analyses still continue to be a mainstay on KidTok.

Figure 5.3. Artist impression of the viral video of the 'Four Seasons Baby' on TikTok and subsequent videos in which sponsors were featured.

A more recent example is TikTok's fascination with the 'Four Seasons Baby'. In the viral video, a mother is heard asking her family 'Who wants to go to the Four Seasons Orlando', to which baby Kate – clad in nappies and carried by her dad – raises her hand and responds with a resounding 'Me!' As with most viral child stars (see chapter 7), the video led to sponsorship and collaboration opportunities for the family – including with the Four Seasons group of hotels. But what is of interest here is the armchair analyses that continue through the networks of conspiracy theories flourishing on TikTok.

Following the viral video, commenters across several platforms began to refer to Kate as a 'fully conscious baby', dissecting her body language frame by frame and offering interpretations as to whether she was developmentally exceptional for her age. In dozens of forums, parents and caregivers contributed experiences with their own children, sincerely debating what the 'normal', 'acceptable', 'average' or 'typical' milestones for babies and toddlers across different age brackets were. Some more enthusiastic threads expended group effort to analyse her fine motor skills, the clarity and diction of her speech, and even the alleged maturity in her eyes. Several news articles picked up on the video, and in their lighthearted stories memorialized Kate as acting 'strangely cognisant' (Masia 2024) and having 'done the seemingly inconceivable' (Scanlan 2024). While this instance of conspiracy theory seems relatively harmful, the practices of armchair analyses and diagnosis are not always so inane, as per 'pandemic babies'.

'#ImJustAKid' Challenge and Memory Lane

'I'm Just A Kid' is the opening line in the chorus of Canadian rock band Simple Plan's 2002 song of the same title. Almost two decades later in 2020, the song experienced a resurgence in popularity when it was used as the audio meme for the popular '#ImJustAKid' Challenge on TikTok. The concept is simple: show the process of your family recreating an old family photograph in the present day, then segue to a screenshot revealing the old family photograph of when you were a child. Bonus points if fidelity is paid to the backdrop, fashion, body language and facial expressions.

For the most part, the Challenge was received with much humour, with reports pointing to 'adults cuddling on their parents' laps' or 'dads giving piggyback rides to their enormous sons' (Locker 2020). The collection of 'throwback' photos was a trip down memory lane, and a nice touch of nostalgia for many now adult TikTokers. Unlike the case studies above, this influx of baby photos volunteered by thousands of people did not appear to spark conversations about the privacy of children and the domestic locus of the home, perhaps because these were adults who exercised agency to post old photos of

Figure 5.4. Artist impression of one of the common posts from the 'I'm Just A Kid' audio meme on TikTok, featuring adults or grown-up children replicating the likeness of old childhood photos.

themselves, and who were not concerned about the misuse of their image. Beyond the nostalgia and the cute, there were some more heartening takes regarding the Challenge.

Clusters of Challenge TikToks took viewers by surprise, as the segue between re-enactments and baby photos demonstrated the successful transition of many trans persons: a transman is seen showing off his mastectomy scars while standing next to two adult women in bikinis on the beach, then the scene segues to three young sisters in bathing suits at a similar beach; an adult woman is cosying up to her parents on a sofa, then the scene segues to a very young boy being sandwiched between his parents on the same couch. The comments sections of these posts often noted minor details, such as how 'happy' the adult trans children were, and how 'accepting' their family must have been considering their 'smiles', 'hugs' and other bodily gestures signalling affection. But there were also limits to the permissibility of intimate body language, especially when the previously endearing poses by young siblings or by parents and their young child are viewed in a different light as adults.

Some of the trending Challenge TikToks that showcased old family photographs of little babies in nappies were re-enacted by adult children clad similarly in their underwear. The trend quickly ventured from 'cute' to 'gross'. In one particular instance, a little baby who was once hugged over the chest by her dad was reiterated as semi-nude young women being cupped at the breasts by her elderly father. These were the TikTok posts that invited nuanced commentary in the comments section, with viewers contemplating how and whether these old baby photographs would be decontextualized and misappropriated by bad faith actors like paedophiles.

When the '#ImJustAKid' Challenge became mainstream, celebrities of all varieties also participated in the trend. It was at this juncture that some of the comments pivoted to gossip, with some childhood photographs of celebrities subject to intense scrutiny. It was not uncommon for fans to fuel speculations that celebrities had undergone plastic surgery or other forms of body modification (Prema 2020). The Challenge culminated in Simple Plan participating themselves, using a greenscreen to bring the five members together to re-enact an old photo from their debut (Smith-Engelhardt 2020).

Conclusion

In May 2023, under my remit as founder of the TikTok Cultures Research Network, I co-hosted the 'TikTok &

Children Symposium' with colleagues. The session included a Fireside Chat with TikTok personnel Claire Gartland, the then Policy Lead for Youth Safety & Wellbeing Global Product, and Kathryn Grant, Outreach & Partnerships Manager. Gartland and Grant's portfolios were nestled under the Trust & Safety arm at TikTok, and they participated to hear firsthand from scholars about the myriad of teething and long-neglected issues facing children who are on TikTok. The Fireside Chat acknowledged the current limits of TikTok's provisions in responding to the wide range of issues, but focused on their efforts towards improving minors' safety and wellbeing, illuminating the backend workings of platform design and user diversity, and assuring the room of the utility of academic research to inform industry advancement (Abidin et al. 2025). More importantly, the conversation also underscored that while changes in platform features and policy always appear to be slow and understandably reactive, as a company TikTok was invested in improving design changes (like daily screen time limits for under-18s) and graduated age-gating options (like Family Pairing) to give its younger users a sense of independence agency within the boundaries of baseline safety. Indeed, emergent scholarship is now focusing on the latent values and utility of TikTok's community guidelines for child users (Turvy 2024), and also assessing whether and how public discourse about TikTok's impact on children 'coincid[es] with significant alterations' to their policies (Ingber and Su 2024: 1).

Perhaps the most sobering iteration of various KidTok child celebrities and trends is still the '#ImJustAKid' Challenge. There were some instances where TikTokers would share heartwarming baby photos, only to segue to pose with urns and funeral portraits, signalling that their loved ones had long passed away. While the comments on such posts often expressed shock – 'That got dark quick'; 'Well now I'm depressed!'; 'This was pretty shocking. . .' – the conversations also reflected upon the genre of KidTok more fondly. Commenters were reflexive about the concerns surrounding the visibility of young children on TikTok, but also cited that the collective archive of baby milestones and childhood memories would serve as a precious chronicle of what growing up in the 2020s was like – and these would be very much cherished some day in the future. This love for memes, and children as memes in particular, is the subject of the next chapter.

6

Meme Celebrities

Introduction

Memes are a major constituent of social media pop cultures: 'the repertoire of communicative, visual, textual and . . . aural artefacts that are popularized by the grassroots, that become instituted as vocabulary and parlance among users, that become critical gateways and entry points for talking about difficult issues' (Abidin and Lee 2022: 8). Early memes were established as textual quips, such as the personal surveys that circulated on the likes of social networking site Friendster ('What is your pet's name? Who is your favourite musician? What is your guilty pleasure?'), or the macro memes featuring white text superimposed on the top and bottom of an image with an animal or person or other object of interest sandwiched in between (think 'LOLcats' at the height of millennial meme culture in the mid-2000s).

Later on, as platforms proliferated and their features and affordances diversified to incorporate different content and formats, memes began to evolve. On YouTube, the digital culture of the early-2010s propelled songs and dances into internationally viral phenomena, spurring tens of thousands of remixed iterations and cover videos as a shared cultural experience (Shifman 2013). The late-2010s culture of short video platforms like TikTok rapidly solidified the 'aural turn' of memes, where audio memes featuring speech, music or other audio would 'take on an intimate disposition, requiring care, tact, and wit to situate and decipher' (Abidin and Kaye 2021: 58).

But beyond their ever-creative formats, memes are also important tools for spotlighting issues in society and for making interventions in important conversations. The humour of memes may be mobilized subversively, such as through apparently uncivil acts of trolling; but even in these spaces, we learn of the important organization and structure of troll groups and how they cultivate and commit to a moral ethos that guides their group behaviour (Phillips 2016). In other words, memes present fertile opportunities for public conversations and for ordinary people to engage in participatory politics (Milner 2018), which have even evidenced productive communal and action-based outcomes for social protests (Mina 2019). In other words, memes can

> maximise entertainment value to encourage audience engagement, strategically deploy refracted publics to circumvent government and/or platform censorship, and multiply social steganography and code-switching to speak to multiple audiences at once. (Abidin and Lee 2022: 22)

In this chapter, I offer a framework for how children progress from being 'meme personalities' to 'meme celebrities', and consider three case studies where meme celebrity children experience different consequences attached to their fame: where 'Jinmiran baby' experienced the unsanctioned profiting off her image; where Gavin Mastodon's cross-cultural popularity in Chinese markets presented the family with rare opportunities to travel on sponsorship; and where the brothers of 'Charlie Bit My Finger' were able to leverage on their once-upon-a-time fame by cashing in on technological developments and updating their relevance as meme celebrities once more.

From 'Meme Personalities' to 'Meme Celebrities'

'Meme personalities' are a subset of memes. They are usually ordinary people who are often '(unwittingly) captured in compromising circumstances or with notable expressions or gestures and become iconized as memes' (Abidin 2018: 44). In other words, meme personalities may include unknowing internet celebrities with no awareness of their online fame and unwilling individuals who find themselves unable to opt out of online visibility. These issues are compounded when it is children and minors who emerge as the memes, and who become a widely recognized internet vernacular and cultural grammar with little autonomy. As such, when children become entangled with the visibility and virality of memes, their likeness and the discourse surrounding it are fruitful avenues for us to think about the implications of online celebrity.

In earlier work studying the taxonomy of internet celebrity, I suggested that there are usually three stages in the life cycle of meme personalities (Abidin 2018: 45–52):

Stage 1, Faces of memes: Photographs of everyday, ordinary people become memorialized for their facial expression, body language or the context of the scene in general, and become widely recognizable when internet users collectively view, remix, circulate and imbue their own meanings onto the image.

Stage 2, Meme personae: People who are behind the 'face of a meme' choose to identify themselves and prolong their fame by recapitulating the discourse and narrative assigned to the meme, either via further role-playing in character through subsequent follow-up memes, or through participation in (often monetized) opportunities that require them to re-enact the meme context.

Stage 3, Meme celebrities: People who once established as 'meme personae' groom their fame into a more sustained, stable and coherent form of online celebrity, usually through the production of new social media contents while continually calling back to the advent of their meme, to solidify the brand of their meme and manage their new careers as vocational public figures.

In the rest of this chapter, we consider case studies where young children have been embroiled in the economy of meme personalities, and the opportunities and consequences when their photograph or video is decontextualized, when their likeness is memorialized as shorthand for a discourse beyond their control, and when their backstories and personal lives appear to be fodder for open conversation online.

'Jinmiran Baby' and Unsanctioned Profiting

In the mid-2010s, reaction gifs and messaging stickers of a Korean toddler began to flood social media. Known only as 'Jinmiran', the baby girl was featured in an array of emotive facial expressions: lips pouting; eyebrows raised; lips pursed around a straw of a packet drink; smiling with eyes closed; frowning with brows burrowed; yawning; falling asleep. Images of the toddler were especially popular on messaging platforms like WhatsApp, WeChat, Line, KakaoTalk, Telegram and Messenger, with entire sticker packs available across a variety of app stores and online sticker maker repositories for download or purchase.

As it turns out, 'Jinmiran' or 'Jin Miran' is not the name of the toddler but of her mother. Based in South Korea, Jinmiran was

Figure 6.1. Artist impression of one of the 'Jinmiran' reaction meme sticker packs that are widely used on messaging apps.

posting updates of everyday life raising her toddler on Korean social media and Instagram when internet users took a swift liking to her especially demonstrative emotional repertoire. Although more popularly known by fans as 'Jinmiran baby', 'Korean sticker baby' or 'Queen of baby stickers', the toddler's name is Rohee. On the likes of sticker maker repositories, gif libraries and social media curations of Rohee's image, she is also variously referred to by the shorthands 'Korean sticker baby', 'the Asian sticker baby' and 'cute sticker baby'; in other words, internet users across geographies, cultures, platforms and formats agreed that she was *the* bona fide face of stickers on the internet.

There are many dedicated pages 'belonging' to Jinmiran. It is often difficult to ascertain the actual ownership and control of these pages because the 'About' and 'Bio' pages variously adopt a first-person stance in their narration, declaring that they are 'the viral Korean meme girl'. The pages also variously claim to be the 'official channels' and 'official pages' of Jinmiran. There are variations like 'official fan pages' and 'main unofficial fan pages', and even country-specific fan pages signalling other types of officialdom, like 'The go-to account for Jinmiran Vietnam fans', 'India official Jinmiran fan page', among others. The followers of these accounts range from thousands to hundreds of thousands of users. On YouTube, these are usually compilations of content from Jinmiran's official social media accounts, curated and sorted by categories such as 'eating and chilling', 'funny', 'dancing', which serve as libraries for fans to take screengrabs and snippets for stickers or gifs. This is evident through the continuous update of existing sticker packs and launch of new ones, each updating the Jinmiran visual lore with newer images.

Despite the rampant (mis)use of Rohee's image, makers and curators of Jinmiran stickers tended to watermark, 'copyright' or claim ownership of their sticker packs, requesting attribution and credit for their curatorial work. It is not uncommon to see downloadable sticker packs with notices like 'These stickers are property of [handle of maker]', or viral Tumblr posts with cautions like 'Please credit [handle of maker] if you use the gif'. Fan reviews on these sticker maker libraries and sticker apps appear to be hungry for more content, with common responses in the vein of 'I want more animated ones', 'very much useful for chats', 'just love this cute baby face'. What is noticeably absent in this discourse is the agency and voice of Rohee and Jinmiran themselves.

In the late-2010s, an assortment of products bearing Rohee's likeness began to proliferate on websites for sale. They include t-shirts, hoodies, tote bags, phone cases, mugs, posters and, of course, actual physical stickers. Although a rare handful of these featured fan art of Rohee, the vast majority were simply bearing screengrabs of her face lifted from Jinmiran's social media. In response, Jinmiran had circulated several notices on different platforms citing the prohibition of unauthorized use of Rohee's likeness. It is unclear how effective these requests were, as they were usually publicized in the Korean language, and translated by the goodwill of a few fans. The unauthorized meme merchandizing of Rohee's likeness led her mother to update her Instagram bio with a notice that has now long stated: 'Prohibition of unauthorized advertising of images and videos [*sic*]'.

Even though she has been in the limelight for almost a decade, there are still hundreds of relatively active social media pages and websites dedicated to Jinmiran. At the time of writing in late-2024, the newest 'Jin Miran' sticker pack was launched on Google Play just a month ago, and dropshipped consumables bearing Rohee's face continue to proliferate on print-on-demand marketplaces for artists like RedBubble. Rohee's younger sister Romi has also begun to enter the ecology of sticker fame, and their mother is currently pregnant with a third child.

'The Internet's Son': Gavin Mastodon and Cross-Cultural Affection

Gavin Mastodon was just two-years-old when his uncle, Nick Mastodon, posted a video of him on Vine. None of this is surprising in the age of sharenting, but the older Mastodon was a Vine internet celebrity whose video brought Gavin more than a toddler's usual fare of online visibility. Through his routine cameos, the younger Mastodon cultivated a following on

Figure 6.2. Artist impression of the Gavin Mastodon meme that is usually used as a reaction sticker or .gif on social media.

Vine and websites began to trace the lore around his popularity with fans (Sweat 2022).

However, it was in 2016 that Mastodon was propelled into viral meme status when tweet threads and dedicated Twitter accounts began to curate images and gifs of his various facial reactions, lifted from Uncle Nick's social media. By then, there was an extensive library of videos capturing Mastodon in 'funny situations', and Olympic athletes and music pop stars alike were referencing him as 'reactions' on their social media (Feldman 2016). Specifically, Mastodon was known for his apt delivery of a facial expression that is best described as 'forcefully smiling through the awkward situation'. By then, he became iconized as 'the Internet's Son' and was also known by his mother's social media handles for his content, 'Gavin Thomas'.

In an interview recounting the years since Mastodon's fame when he turned ten, his mother recounted that '[d]espite his immense online fandom, Gavin has led a pretty normal life to any other kid growing up'. This seems like a humble claim considering that Mastodon's meme celebrity has taken the Minnesota-based family to New York and Los Angeles for appearances, and that he is wildly popular all the way to China (Schwartz 2019).

Known better as 'Fake Smile Boy' in China, Mastodon is well loved on Chinese social media as a popular template for macros memes bearing Chinese-language texts that describe a variety of difficult situations in life. He launched his Weibo account in 2018, the micro-blogging platform where users had long curated memes of him. Mastodon has been invited to China twice to guest on television and appear at events (Chen 2018). At age seven, he was taken on a tour of notable Chinese landmarks like the Forbidden City in Beijing, and asked to re-enact his signature 'awkward smile' while dressed in traditional Chinese attire (CGTN 2018). Local Chinese reports point out that his thousands of fans interpreted his meme as 'polite but reluctant', which was a 'very relatable emotion' in their cultural setting (CGTN 2018).

Like many children who are meme celebrities, Mastodon's image is often deconstructed and decontextualized in a variety of conversations online. In this instance, given the difference in cultures and languages between American and Chinese social media, the context is even further removed. My digital ethnography has surfaced the use of Mastodon as a reaction gif in some NSFW English-language threads, and it was alarming to see the image of a child nestled within the comments sections and online fora of more adult contents. However, in China his awkward smile continues to symbolize an expressive discourse for adults who are navigating difficult topics, and is often used as a closing statement to exit from awkward conversations. In 2021, Mastodon's mother announced on Twitter that 'after extensively researching the industry' they had decided to launch Gavin NFTs (non-fungible tokens) as 'a fun way to contribute to Gavin's future', presumably setting aside earnings for his college fund (Sweat 2022).

The Brothers of 'Charlie Bit My Finger' and Resurging Relevance

In 2021, the brothers of the 2007 YouTube meme 'Charlie Bit My Finger' surfaced in the news after more than a decade, as the parents of baby Charlie and older brother Harry sold their video clip as an NFT. Having amassed over 885 million views on YouTube alone at the time of the sale, the meme is beloved by many on the internet. But at fourteen-years-old then, the video was posted too early in nascent digital cultures and could not capitalize upon the flourishing meme industry as it is today. For a price tag of GB £500,000 (Evans 2021), the family was glad to be able to make some money off their viral meme in an auction, in 'the perfect opportunity to embrace the next iteration of the internet' (Bowman 2021). The then fifteen- and seventeen-year-old brothers declared their intention to use some of the profits to fund their university education (Evans 2021). However, fans of the beloved meme felt differently.

Shortly after the sale, the family announced that the video would be deleted from YouTube as it was now private

Figure 6.3. Artist impression of the brothers known for the popular 'Charlie Bit My Finger' meme video on YouTube.

property, with the original copy being owned by the highest bidder (Bowman 2021). The news was received with an uproar, with hundreds of comment threads, commentaries and news editorials pondering over the ownership of meme celebrity. It was the public that made Charlie and Harry meme celebrities. It was the public's views and streams that assigned the meme video a value. How could this now all be 'owned' by a private bidder overnight? Following the protest, the family announced that after consultation with the buyer, they had decided to retain the video on YouTube as 'an important part of popular culture' (Nover 2021). And thus, through this story of opportune monetization came an important news cycle illuminating the cautionary tale to pay homage and gratitude to the people who make meme celebrities overnight: the internet public.

Conclusion

The case studies above evidence the different opportunities, consequences and at times unanticipated outcomes experienced by children and their families when they become instituted as meme celebrities. Reflecting the vast economic potential of the meme economy, many of the critical decisions made by the guardians of these children involve calculated decisions about balancing visibility, relevance and overexposure, in a delicate dance between making the best of an opportunity and plain exploitation. Given their early start as memes, many of the children who go on to be meme personae or meme celebrities focus their content production on the theme of their initial fame, and thus do not (have to) volunteer as much of their private lives as other types of child Influencers. While these limit the possible advantages of visibility – whether charity, awareness raising or monetization – there are also instances where the time and tide of technology shift so much that these meme celebrities enter into relevance again. In the next chapter, we consider an even more unpredictable and time-sensitive mode of internet fame through the instance of 'Viral Stars'.

7

Viral Stars

Introduction

In September 2022, social media were swamped with reposts of a little boy exclaiming his love for corn: 'It's corn!', 'Have a cornstastic day!' The source is an eighty-five-second Instagram clip. The protagonist is seven-year-old Tariq from the USA. His viral interview, and a myriad of creative remixes of it, have been reshared across Instagram, YouTube, Twitter, and most notably TikTok, where he has become an audio meme (see chapter 6). And on the strength of his accidental virality, 'Corn Kid' went on to feature in a string of content collaborations with notable Influencers (like MrBeast) and brands (like Chipotle) (Abidin 2022). It was not long before a dedicated Cameo account was launched in his name – the video-sharing platform where users can pay to send private messages to internet celebrities or request personalized video messages (Corn Kid 2022).

'Corn Kid' is an example of a viral star, and an exemplar of how 'everyday users in organically viral social media posts, especially those involving young children and teenagers, become systemically absorbed, groomed, and even exploited

Figure 7.1. Artist impression of Tariq, who is known as the viral 'Corn Kid' on TikTok and YouTube.

by the mainstream media into traditional celebrity icons' (Abidin 2018: 56). Guardians of viral children will often find themselves in a world of instantaneous opportunity, as offers of paid cameos, corporate partnerships, talent brokerage and even child Influencer contracts may line up. Depending on the extent of the virality and how mineable the initial piece of content is, the initial payout can range from the low thousands to the high tens of thousands.

But as I note in an editorial pointing to under-considered concerns when kids go viral (Abidin 2022), the immediate moment following instant fame is the most crucial for important decisions. And when the offers are so tantalizing and transient, given the wavering interest of the public and the usually short-lived cycles of online virality, guardians are pressured to make very quick decisions. It is in these moments where guardians may have little headspace to consider whether the offers of advertising placements are child-friendly or if they align with their own family values; whether the compensation they are offered is fair; whether the continued visibility of their viral child may usher in unforeseen consequences; and indeed whether the child may even enjoy this prolonged exposure to online virality and visibility. This becomes all the more pressing when TV talk show circuits enter the playing field.

In her study of American TV talk shows, sociologist Laura Grindstaff (2002) offers the concept of 'the money shot' to explain how despite the allowance of sharing the spotlight with 'ordinary people' and their 'real stories', producers tended to elicit only the most 'dramatic performances' from their guests and frame them in specific ways that solicit judgement from viewers. It is thus no surprise that American talk shows are well known for featuring – or even creating – social media viral children to guest on episodes, at times placing them in compromising positions. In this chapter, we will review how American talk show circuits tend to draw on the social media labour and contents of children for their programming; take a detailed look at *The Ellen DeGeneres Show* as an instance of how children who are 'Viral Stars' become systematically absorbed and exploited by the traditional entertainment industry; and consider a brief case study of how 'Viral Stars' are differently managed by child actor and child idol agencies which come under tighter jurisdiction in the South Korean market.

Talk Show Circuits

In prior work tracing the relationship between internet celebrity and traditional media, I note that TV talk shows often 'mine the creative labour of internet users as fodder for prime-time television' (Abidin 2018: 56). From *The Tonight Show Starring Jimmy Fallon*'s 'Hashtag Fail' segment (@fallontonight 2012) to *Jimmy Kimmel Live!*'s 'I told my kids I ate all their Halloween

Figure 7.2. Artist impression of the 'Tell your kids you ate all their candy' Halloween prank meme from the Jimmy Kimmel show on YouTube.

candy' video challenge (@JimmyKimmelLive 2011), TV talk shows have been soliciting the free (and usually willing) labour of social media users to produce content for their show.

Among the offerings of these American TV talk shows, *The Ellen DeGeneres Show* appears to have systematically mined for and continued to groom 'a brigade of viral child stars' in a model of production that I have called 'The Ellen Factory' (Abidin 2018: 57). As such, the Show and some of its most renowned viral child stars will be the focus of this chapter. When it launched in 2003, *The Ellen DeGeneres Show* was notably different than the following discussions will point to, having focused on kindness and positivity. The Show often curated segments that featured 'feel good' trends or 'heart-warming' moments first discovered on social media, to celebrate humanity and provide a backstory to the instance of social media virality. These would often include sit-down interviews with families in need whose stories were spotlighted on social media, and offers of charity through sponsored cheques or gifts made available through the Show's advertisers.

Later on, the Show appeared to shift its focus to the young children who attain virality online, usually inviting them as guests on the Show for an interview and a performance to replicate their viral act for a live audience. The intense public visibility of these young children would be perpetuated, as clips of the Show would themselves attain virality online, and select viral child stars would be given recurring segments on the Show as returning guests. However, as generations of viral child stars grow up 'extremely online' via the model of *The Ellen DeGeneres Show*, they appear to experience uneven benefits and consequences even a decade after their first brush with fame.

The 'Ellen' Production of Sophia Grace & Rosie

The trajectory and progress of British cousins Sophia Grace Brownlee and Rosie McClelland is especially interesting to study. The pair first went viral on YouTube in 2011 at the ages of eight and five for covering Nicki Minaj's 'Super Bass', and were subsequently groomed by 'The Ellen Factory' into multi-platform celebrities in both the social media and traditional entertainment industries. The more than half a billion views that Sophia Grace & Rosie brought to the Ellen YouTube channel is of significant economic value and continues to attract views even though the show itself has ended. As the two girls grow to become adults, their legacy and identities appear indefinitely and inextricably linked to their television show appearances.

This section considers their initial foray into digital media spaces, the precise crux of their internet virality, their first appearances and subsequent cooptation into *The Ellen DeGeneres Show*, and the management of their viral stardom and their digital estates as part of a networked production of child celebrity. I offer a schema of seven milestones tracking how young children transit from viral video fame on social

Figure 7.3. Artist impression of Sophia Grace & Rosie, who first became viral while dressed in ballet tutus in YouTube videos, and who re-enacted their notable ballet tutu fashion as older teens years later.

media to traditional celebrity in the mainstream entertainment industry: Viral happenstance; Television debut; Branded grooming; Intimacy maintenance; Digital estate expansion; Influencer career transition; and Paying homage.

Viral happenstance

Sophia Grace Brownlee (b. 2003) and Rosie McClelland (b. 2006) are a pair of cousins from Essex, England. Better known on the internet as 'Sophia Grace & Rosie', the duo went viral on YouTube at ages eight and five when Sophia Grace's mother uploaded a video of the girls singing Nicki Minaj's 'Super Bass' in September 2011 (@SophiaGrace 2011a). The viral video was the debut post on the YouTube channel 'Sophia Grace', and has accumulated over 55 million views as of September 2023.

Television debut

After a month of ongoing online virality, in October 2011, *The Ellen DeGeneres Show* flew the cousins to the US for an exclusive interview with show host Ellen, where they were also asked to re-enact their viral performance to a live audience (@TheEllenShow 2011a). After expressing their great love for Nicki Minaj, the rapper appeared on stage to the girls' surprise, even agreeing to sing the iconic now-viral song with them (@TheEllenShow 2011b). As of September 2023, the videos have recorded over 47 million and over 150 million views respectively (@TheEllenShow 2011a, 2011b).

Branded grooming

Thanks to the live studio recording being cross-posted on *The Ellen DeGeneres Show*'s YouTube channel, the young girls experienced extended virality on YouTube. In the wake of this, the TV show subsequently published previously unseen behind-the-scenes footage of Sophia Grace & Rosie from the recording session (@TheEllenShow 2011c), in a bid to capitalize upon their virality and extend their shelf life. It was not long before the girls were formally introduced as recurring 'characters' on *The Ellen DeGeneres Show*, representing the

TV show at various red carpet events (@TheEllenShow 2011d, 2011e, 2012a, 2013a), and even starring in vlogs showcasing sponsored brands on the TV show's YouTube channel, including Target (@TheEllenShow 2012b), Fijit, (@TheEllenShow 2012c) and Disney (@TheEllenShow 2013b).

Eventually, Sophia Grace & Rosie became a staple in the programming of the Show, with a dedicated segment that they would host known as '"Tea Time" with Sophia Grace & Rosie'. Eight episodes were published between September 2012 and May 2013 (@TheEllenShow 2013c), and all subsequently went viral on YouTube as well. The strategic spotting, grooming and institutionalization of the young viral stars by *The Ellen DeGeneres Show* demonstrate an effective trajectory for talent scouting, and even expanding the online reputation of the TV show via its YouTube engagements. This was especially evident when Sophia Grace & Rosie were invited back to the show to celebrate their 100 millionth view on YouTube (@TheEllenShow 2012d). In subsequent years, they also released their own book and movie, produced by *The Ellen DeGeneres Show* (@TheEllenShow 2013d, 2014a).

Intimacy maintenance

However, to avoid the risk of being 'sell-outs', producers would regularly invite Sophia Grace & Rosie back on *The Ellen DeGeneres Show* to chat about their personal lives, using 'authenticity' as a narrative device to reinstall public perception that they were ordinary children after all (Abidin 2017a). These episodes included show segments of their experiences as Britons regularly visiting America (@TheEllenShow 2012e), on their dream jobs (@TheEllenShow 2013e) and their family life (@TheEllenShow 2013f, 2014b). Whenever there was a lull in branded content engagements or a lack of 'TV worthy' updates in their personal lives, the girls were brought back on the Show (@TheEllenShow 2013g, 2014c, 2015) simply to maintain their visibility with audiences and to maintain content production for the Show's YouTube channel, including the curation of behind-the-scenes footage (@TheEllenShow 2012f, 2012g, 2012h) to foster a sense of ongoing connection (Abidin 2016). All content featuring Sophia Grace & Rosie on *The Ellen DeGeneres Show* has been streamed into a playlist on their YouTube channel (TheEllenShow 2013e) and website (Ellen 2017).

Digital estate expansion

As the years passed and the cousins approached teenhood, it became clear that the social media presence of Sophia Grace was more intentionally curated and branded for a career in the (internet) entertainment industry while Rosie faded into the background for some years, only to launch her own YouTube foray into a musical career in her mid-teens in 2018. Aside from the structural expansion of rebranding her YouTube channel to focus on Sophia Grace rather than the duo (@SophiaGrace 2011b) and starting a Facebook page as 'Sophia Grace The Artist' (SophiaGraceTheArtist n.d.), Sophia Grace's digital estates also underwent content expansion as she began to produce her own music (@SophiaGrace 2013, 2015), meet mainstream entertainment industry celebrities (@SophiaGrace 2011c) and collaborate with fellow internet celebrities (Zamolo 2017; @JessiiVee 2017; @SophiaGrace 2016a).

Influencer career transition

Since turning thirteen in 2016, Sophia Grace formally launched her Influencer career by engaging in Influencer content vernacular and YouTube tropes. These include participating in internet viral trends unrelated to her music career, such as making slime (@SophiaGrace 2017a) and the Oreo challenge (@SophiaGrace 2017b), engaging in the attention economy of clickbait such as

Q&As addressing her budding romantic life (@SophiaGrace 2017c) and expanding her presence in other genres on YouTube such as makeup tutorials (@SophiaGrace 2017d). In order to maintain her sense of relatability with audiences, Sophia Grace has also been producing vlogs in the YouTube vernacular to publicize her domestic spaces and private life, including bedroom chats (@SophiaGrace 2016b), her morning routine (@SophiaGrace 2016c), the travelogue (@SophiaGrace 2016d), more personalized Q&As (@SophiaGrace 2016e) and potentially a proximate micro-celebrification of her young sister, Belle, who made a debut in one of Sophia Grace's vlogs (@SophiaGrace 2016f). By September 2023, Sophia Grace boasted over 190 videos on her YouTube channel, with over 3.5 million subscribers, which is sustained at the time of writing.

Paying homage

Sophia Grace (& Rosie)'s acknowledgement of *The Ellen DeGeneres Show* as the springboard for their expanded and extended fame post-virality is evident in several of their public messages, including their movie trailer, which introduces the girls as 'You know them from *The Ellen DeGeneres Show*' (@TheEllenShow 2013d, 2014a). However, *The Ellen DeGeneres Show* and similar TV talk show formats have no doubt opportunistically capitalized upon the social capital of such viral video children by harnessing their fame and packaging it into more accessible, commercial and deliberate consumption bytes. In the trajectory of viral video children, the crucial milestone is the period between 'viral happenstance' and 'television debut' wherein networks scramble to book the latest internet sensation in order to secure their mainstream media debut and associate their TV brand with the child's subsequent amplification across platforms and media. And it is at the 'branded grooming' stage that TV networks convert the social capital of their viral child assets into economic capital.

To avoid the risk of being sell-outs and losing public interest, the 'intimacy maintenance' stage is crucial to continually reassert these viral child stars' statuses as ordinary children who were discovered by happenstance, while simultaneously and subtly continuing to groom them into the stage of 'digital estate expansion', and eventually 'Influencer career transition. So successful is this model of viral kid celebrity pathway that *The Ellen DeGeneres Show* has curated its own series of adorable kids in a playlist of over 200 videos with such viral children engaging in various (commercial) activities on the Show (@TheEllenShow n.d.). This eventually culminated in Ellen DeGeneres' collaboration with television network NBC to produce the talk show *Little Big Shots*, which is dedicated to televising the childlike quips, talents and reactions of ordinary children usually discovered through social media (NBC n.d.).

Ellen's Curtain Call (Or Not)

When *The Ellen DeGeneres Show* produced its final season in 2022, many episodes revisited favourite celebrities and guests, usually framed with nostalgic packages of their earlier visits to the Show. On 12 May 2022, Sophia Grace and Rosie made their final return to the 'mothership', once again sitting on Ellen's sofa wearing tutus, introduced by a package featuring clips from their many earlier appearances, but swiftly moving past the fact they had not been on the Show for nearly six years. While the broadcast of the Show ended, its main YouTube channel still pumps out clips and historical content, as well as re-curating popular past clips. Notably, the videos in the playlist 'Sophia Grace and Rosie on Ellen', which features 77 videos of their appearances on the show, has cumulatively had over 650 million views as of September 2023, and continues to attract a nostalgic audience. The Show's last episode was broadcast in May 2022, but the YouTube playlist featuring the girls was still being updated and expanded in January 2023, highlighting the value of curating and re-curating this content for continued viewership.

While it could be argued that their appearances on Ellen were mutually beneficial in that there was a symbiotic relationship potentially amplifying the girls' fame, once the show wrapped the only lingering relationship is parasitic, continuing to extract views of historic content in the long tail of the show in online segments. Even after the broadcasts have ended, the two young girls continue to attract views, and presumably advertising revenue, for *The Ellen DeGeneres Show*. Indeed, on 30 June 2023 the Ellen DeGeneres team posted a video collage of a number of Sophia Grace & Rosie's 2012 and 2013 TV appearances on her Instagram account with the caption 'Tea Time is Cuter with Tutus. Watch Every Episode of Tea Time With @therealsophiagrace & @rosiergm on my YouTube channel' (@ellendegeneres 2023), explicitly continuing this parasitic practice via another social media platform.

Several months after her final Ellen appearance in May 2022 Sophia Grace announced on her own YouTube channel that she was pregnant, sharing the first ultrasound photo and teasing audiences that they would have to return at a later date for a 'gender reveal' announcement (@SophiaGrace 2022). When her story was picked up by popular magazines, they routinely referred to her as an '"Ellen DeGeneres Show" Star' (e.g. Blanchet 2022). After her child was born, Sophia Grace continued to be framed by her appearances on *The Ellen DeGeneres Show*, with the likes of *E! News* noting 'Sophia Grace, who rose to fame as a YouTube sensation and child star on *The Ellen DeGeneres Show*, has welcomed her first child' (Heller 2023). Moreover, when Sophia Grace posted the news of her son's birth on Instagram (@therealsophiagrace 2023), the two most prominent and liked comments were from Ellen DeGeneres and Rosie McClelland, with Ellen's comment itself receiving over 22,000 likes as of the time of data collection in September

2023. Despite the curtain call of *The Ellen DeGeneres Show*, it appears that the far-reaching tentacles of 'The Ellen Factory' continue to proliferate.

Virality with Protections: Park Geon Roung, the 'Baby Shark' Boy

The 'Baby Shark Dance' video was published on YouTube in 2016, featuring two young children in costume dancing alongside an animated family of sharks to the sounds of a very catchy song. Owing to it being an earworm, the video quickly amassed millions of views, sending the two children – child actors Park Geon Roung and Elaine Kim Johnston – into viral stardom (Lim 2024). At the time of writing, the 'Baby Shark Dance' video has accumulated 15 billion views on YouTube (Cord-Cruz et al. 2024).

However, as the music video was produced by an education brand Pinkfong, owned by South Korean company SmartStudy, the child actors featured were managed by an agency. As such, despite this instantaneous international virality, the children's subsequent activities still largely remained within the remit of their company as models and actors on Pinkfong's YouTube channels. There are only a handful of news articles and fan-produced wiki profiles that have looked into the background and identities of the 'Baby Shark' children, and for a long time the only information that was widely public was their names. In 2024, a few news articles spotlighted the now fifteen-year-old Park, and through screengrabs of his social media celebrated him for his good looks as a teenager (e.g. Cord-Cruz et al. 2024; Lim 2024). Park is reportedly a member of a 'kids K-pop band' known as 'Play With Me Club' (Lim 2024). Said 'kids K-pop band' was the subject of a recent study by collaborators and I (Lee et al. 2024) looking into the phenomenon of 'kids-dol' (키즈돌) or 'child idols' in the Korean market. As such, despite

Figure 7.4. Artist impression of Park Geon Roung, who first became viral for starring in the 'Baby Shark' music video as a child in 2016, and who became viral again when new images of him circulated online in 2024.

having been entangled with global social media virality on a massive scale, not much else was known about Park's personal life as a child as his welfare was then under the remit of his talent agency and now under the remit of his kids-dol agency; both of these are in turn under the governance of Korean law regulating the protection of child actors and performers.

Conclusion

Readers may have noticed that the case studies presented in this chapter have focused heavily on viral child stars as they are embroiled in the American media industries. This is in part due to the older legacies of TV talk show circuits in the US, and the ability to expend resources to front stage international acts (like British cousins Sophia Grace & Rosie). In my recent body of work, I have been focused on the Korean entertainment industries, conducting various studies on the implications of social media visibility of young children. For instance, there is an established route for social media viral children to be quickly signed to talent agencies, where they will train to be artists in the K-pop industry (Lee and Abidin 2023). In doing so, these children come under the jurisdiction of the law governing the traditional entertainment industries, which are structured and extensive. In other words, it is important to consider how different media ecologies and local markets manage viral child stars differently, especially considering the different provisions by industry and regulations by law. The next chapter considers how children are involved in the media industry as variety stars.

8

Variety Stars

Introduction

Since 2016, I have been studying different forms of child internet celebrities in the Korean market (see case study of guitar prodigy Sungha Jung in Abidin 2018). At the Korean Studies Association of Australasia (KSAA) Biennial Conference in 2019, I had the opportunity to present some early findings on how some K-pop companies appear to be relying on children and young talents for cross-cultural promotion between Korea and North America, specifically through YouTube and Instagram contents (Abidin 2019). A year later, at the plenary for the Fan Studies Network North America (FSNNA) Conference in 2020, I was invited to share preliminary analysis on how K-pop was shaping politics and digital influence in fandoms, and spotlighted case studies focused on very young child stars who were being absorbed into the Influencer industry following very successful appearances on Korean variety-reality TV programmes (Larsen et al. 2020). Later on, in collaboration with media studies scholar Jin Lee, we worked on a series of interconnected projects locating the place of children in the wider Korean entertainment and social media industries.

For instance, we have considered how young audiences were roped in as fans through campaigns like TikTok Stage and TikTok dance challenges to successfully platform TikTok into the Korean market (Abidin and Lee 2023), and the presence and discourse of children in the mixed-race relationships of *oegugin* (foreigner) Influencers (Lee and Abidin 2022). This chapter considers another iteration, looking at how children who are stars of variety shows in the Korean entertainment industry present a different form of 'internet famous' children. I study the reality TV shows *The Return of Superman* and *Half-Moon Friends* to understand how the domestic Korean television market and international fandom across social media intertwine to extend the internet fame of variety star children, and extend opportunities for sponsored messages, whether political or commercial.

Seungjae in 'The Return of Superman'

The Return of Superman (TROS) is a variety reality TV show launched in September 2013 by the Korean Broadcasting System (KBS) network, which documents 'a day in the life' of male South Korean celebrities who become primary caregivers for their young children over a period of forty-eight hours (usually the weekend) while their wives 'take a break'. Among the many children who become breakout stars on the show is Ko Seungjae, who first debuted on the series as a two-year-old in November 2016 before retiring from the show in June 2019. The series also features his celebrity father, Ko Jiyong from the first-generation K-pop idol group Sech Kies. The group was active between 1997 and 2000 before taking a break, then regrouped to continue producing music and performing in 2016 to 2021.

Seungjae and Jiyong are a well-loved duo on the show, with fans spanning international markets. Below, we consider some

Figure 8.1. Artist impression of a scene featuring child star Seungjae and his father Ko Jiyong, who appeared on several episodes in *The Return of Superman* TV series, depicting Seungjae completing everyday errands while a hidden camera filmed him.

of the recurring narratives in the series through several examples to understand how Seungjae has been portrayed, which led to an expansive and growing fandom fawning over him between the ages of two- and five-years-old. Please note that full episodes were available on the free-to-air channel KBS World TV during broadcast, when data collection took place. However, the broadcaster has also made select snippets of the show publicly accessible on their official YouTube channel, which will be cited below wherever possible.

The filial son

Given that the premise of the series is the solo parenting adventures of celebrity fathers, many of the plotlines involve humorous moments between Seungjae and Jiyong. In the snippet 'Seungjae pours water into his dad to cure his hangover!' (@kbsworldtv 2017a), Jiyong is nursing a headache from a hangover and is seen lying down on the living room floor. He groans and moans, but these expressions are no doubt exaggerated to solicit a response from Seungjae and for the camera. The camera crew, who are hidden behind curtains and inside tents attempting to camouflage with the interior decor of the house, repeatedly zoom in on Seungjae, as the audience sees close-ups of his face appearing concerned, afraid and contemplative. In the scene, Seungjae is seen repeatedly walking up to his father to offer him various comforts – a toy, a blanket, some snacks. A voiceover by a disembodied commentator in the studio points out that Seungjae is a filial little boy for showing care towards his father, and marvels at how he already has a strong bond with his father at such a young age. Eventually, Seungjae fetches a cup of water and pours it over his father's head to freshen him up. Jiyong is caught off-guard, he gets up from the floor, cleans himself up, but thanks Seungjae for (literally) showering his father with care and affection.

The kind child

There are also several episodes that stage social experiments to gauge Seungjae's reactions to a series of scenarios. One example is 'Seungjae's tears for the beggar hyungs "I'm going to feed them"' (@kbsworldtv 2017b), where a pair of men dress up in rags and pretend to be hungry beggars soliciting food from Seungjae at a restaurant. The camera consistently pans to Seungjae's face, focusing on the tears welling up in his eyes, and the voiceover points out the obvious to the audience:

Seungjae is about to burst into tears, his voice is wavering, his little hands are trembling, his bodily posture continually turns to face the 'beggars' and he is inching closer to them. The narration underscores Seungjae's empathy, as he offers them food from his table, and tells them – through toddler tears and fears – that he wants them to be fine, fed and healthy. Other episodes feature Seungjae out running errands with Jiyong, or going on fun excursions. These everyday moments capture the micro-expressions and gestures that Seungjae displays, at times over-analysing little moments and turns of speech through replays of select highlights. For example, in a scene where he is putting little crabs into a fish tank, he pleads with the fish not to eat the crabs (@kbsworldtv 2017c), and the episode shows how he learns about care and responsibility for his temporary 'pets'.

The friendly collaborator

Because the TV series is ultimately a commercial project, there are instances of collaborations strategically placed in the episodes. Though not strictly product placement or overt marketing like the examples discussed previously (see chapter 2), the promotional nature of the contents is still evident. For example, in 'Seungjae's linguistic skills that surprised everyone' (@kbsworldtv 2017d) a child development expert is spotlighted as she contributes as a guest commentator for the episode to share opinions on Seungjae's developed language skills; and in 'Seungjae finally reunites with Uncle Liu Yihao in Taiwan!!' (@kbsworldtv 2018a) the child stars in yet another episode featuring recurring guest musician Liu Yihao from Taiwan as part of a longer stream of collaborations between the Korean and Taiwanese pop markets.

The young patriot

In other episodes, Seungjae appears to be depicted as part of larger nationalist projects or discourse despite his young age. 'Selling empty bottles to buy ice-cream!!!' (@kbsworldtv 2017e) sees the three-year-old struggling with several empty plastic bottles and bags collected for recycling, as his little hands and arms stretch to gather as many as he can (albeit clumsily) to deposit at a recycling kiosk. Seungjae is motivated to do so because his dad reminds him that the loose change he collects from the deposit will fund his snacks for the day. In doing so, the series also inserts brief reminders throughout the episode – through the voiceover narration, layover text on screen and captions – of how easy it is to recycle, encouraging viewers to do so as well. In yet another episode, Seungjae visits Dokdo Island with his father and learns about the history of the place. Dokdo Island is a contested territory, as Japan once colonized it from Korea, and has in the past attempted to claim ownership over it. In 'Seungjae "Please take good care of Dokdo Island ♥"' (@kbsworldtv 2018b), the little boy runs into a group of mostly senior citizens on a tour towards the end of his excursion with his father. They wave small Korean flags, and are gathered in a group behind a larger flag for their photo opportunity. Seungjae and Jiyong post for a photo with the group, when they break out in song about Dokdo Island being their land. The song is lengthy and wordy at five verses, the group is very impressed with Seungjae for his memory and eloquence, but the meta-commentary of the episode expresses further appreciation for young Seungjae's love for his country, and his exemplar as a patriot on national TV – at all of four-years-old.

The Children of *Half-Moon Friends*

Half-Moon Friends (HMF) – or *Bandalchingu* (반달친구) – is a limited-run variety reality TV show airing between April and July 2016, featuring K-pop idol group WINNER running a daycare centre for ten children over two weeks. At the time of data collection (and at writing), full episodes are paywalled and publicly-accessible versions are reposts on pirated sites or unauthorized fan uploads. As such, please note that the discussions below do not include in-text references to the source materials. However, the official broadcaster of the series, JTBC Entertainment, has curated a series of short highlights from the episodes that continue to be publicly-accessible on their YouTube channel (JTBC Entertainment 2016). Among the breakout stars of the show are siblings Minjoon and Jei, who were six- and four-years-old respectively at the time of filming. This section considers the three eras of content programming on Minjoon and Jei's mother's Instagram account, which saw the children progress from variety stars to family Influencers.

Show promos

Following the debut of HMF on air, viewers took to searching for social media profiles of the children. As a seasoned variety show fan, I knew the local forums at which to gather, to retrieve information from the more enthusiastic and hardworking fans who would have already done the curatorial work of gathering lists of these profiles and additional biographical information about the cast. I began following some of these cast members early into the lifespan of the programme. Across the four months of the show's broadcast, I observed that some parents of the children began to 'professionalize' their accounts, as they saw a swift rise in followers and international attention funnelled towards them within a very short span of time. This included 'cleaning up' their accounts by deleting or making private select pictures, such as ones revealing the location or interior of their homes, photos with other family members, or any identifying details of their children and family. It was also during this time where many of the parents took to promoting the show, or commenting on episodes, in direct response to comments from international fans.

For Stella, the mother of Minjoon and Jei, one of the early 'show promo' posts was a digital poster of Jei from the show, profiling her as being aged four, and listing some of her quirks, like enjoying good food. Other posts feature screengrabs from the show, with captions providing narration as further context or as parasocial material to interact with fans. For example, a screengrab of Jei from an episode shows her looking uncertain on screen; the larger context of the episode sees her briefly contemplating what she should do and where she should go, as the older six- and seven-year-olds in the room appear to be more confident. Stella captions her Instagram post to say that this was Jei's classic look of uncertainty, finding humour in the moment as the close-up of her facial expression was especially adorable. The captions end with a string of 'official hashtags' used by both the show and the K-pop idol group, and some 'unofficial hashtags' popularized by fans. An example of the latter is '#EatingFairy' (translated from the Korean language), which continues to be Jei's nickname on the show. Still a third group of captions are drawn from popular social media trends, like '#ParentingInstagram' (translated from the Korean language).

Post-show breadcrumbs

After HMF ended its run, many parents shared snippets that featured behind-the-scenes of the production, presumably because they now had permission to do so. One of Stella's posts was a 'class photograph' of all the children clad in their daycare uniform and posing with the idol group. Her captions

Figure 8.2. Artist impression of Minjoon and Jei, who starred in the *Half-Moon Friends* variety show where they attended a daycare centre run by K-pop idols, and who continued to meet with the idols as older children long after the show had ended.

include a bittersweet farewell to the show, and gratitude to the fans (e.g. 'ThankYouBandalFriends') who have made the experience so special for the children and family through their affection online. Many parents published posts to the same effect. However, the 'post-show breadcrumbs' continued for up to two years after the last episode, as many parents shared snippets of their children 'reuniting' with the pop group at various events in official and non-official capacities.

In 2018, two years following the broadcast, Minjoon and Jei are seen in a photograph with one of the idol-teachers, Mino, at his Leica photo exhibition. Mino is positioned in the centre, embracing a child in each arm. The photo was posted on Stella's Instagram account, and swiftly reposted on several news sites, fan sites and fan forums that continue to show interest in the show. Comments reveal that fans are 'still rewatching episodes' of their beloved series, and 'so surprised' to see how well the children have grown up. Despite the years since the show ended, the 'post-show breadcrumbs' mainly produced by the parents on social media continue to invoke interest in fans – of the children, of the idols and of the show – and these occasional direct exchanges between the cast appear to reinforce a mutual reminiscing and nostalgia for their brief time shared together.

Pivoting to family influencers

My digital ethnography noted that shortly after the conclusion of the show, many parents who had experienced a rapid growth in their Instagram followings began to feature some paid content. These include health supplements for their children, children's clothes, educational materials, and also family-friendly events and exhibitions. In other words, many of them were pivoting from variety show stars to family Influencers (see chapter 3). At the time of my data collection in 2019, Stella's Instagram account featured over 40,600 followers across over 1,500 posts, and her Instagram bio states: 'The exciting daily life of Half-Moon Friends Jeon Min-jun and Jeon Jae-i [*sic*]' [translated from the Korean]. Stella's Instagram began to feature her husband more, and the family of four are documented engaging in everyday activities and outings.

I had the privilege to meet with Stella in person during fieldwork in Seoul in 2019, and learnt about the family's experience with raising 'internet famous' children. Stella recounted to me the details behind how her children were recruited for the programme, their ongoing friendship with the K-pop idols, and how the family was balancing their 'personal time' and 'working time' as they continue as family Influencers. She tells me that while her children were initially befuddled by fans who would approach them on the street, this occurred more when they were younger at ages four and six, and so they did not think much of it and do not have a very active memory of being 'famous' to strangers. She explains that her children were told to be appreciative towards these fans, to thank them for their 'love', but to also know that they were always 'physically safe' as mom or dad were right by their side to watch out for them.

At the time of our meeting, the children are seven- and nine-years-old; I ask if their classmates in school know about their childhood fame. Stella reveals that some classmates recall the show and recognize her children as cast members, but the curiosity does not last long as 'kids are kids after all', with 'short lived attention spans', and that Minjoon and Jei generally live very 'normal childhoods'.

I press Stella a little further and ask about what it is like to be a 'momager' (mom-manager) for her family Influencer unit. She tells me that as she and her husband have full-time jobs, they only engage in family Influencer opportunities occasionally, and only if the offer is very appealing to them. She is in contact with other parents from the show and has also gleaned knowledge about how other parents manage their child Influencers, but does not intend for Minjoon and Jei to pursue child celebrity any further than their variety show features in early childhood. When the children were younger and they received more invitations to event appearances or to shoot/film sponsored contents, Stella would make the effort to negotiate the contracts to include a no-show clause, to cover unforeseen circumstances that might delay or cancel their involvement in sponsored activities, such as poor health or the children's disinterest. She felt it was important for clients to understand that she was a parent first, manager second, and would only take up assignments that contractually prioritized the wellbeing of her children. While some offers were retracted due to her requirements, for the most part she says the family has had a great experience with their sponsored engagements.

Life as per normal

Now that her children are older, I jokingly ask if they are still 'compliant' with mom's arrangements. She transparently reveals that when they were younger, her children once expressed being 'tired' that every weekend seemed to be occupied with an activity, whether for a client or 'for the 'gram' – that is, engaging in a family activity with some intention to produce content for their social media. That was a turning point for her, and she has since managed the family calendar to have regular downtime. She also explains that as Minjoon and Jei grow older, they are 'ageing out' of the 'cute category', and the frequency and nature of sponsored opportunities has changed; at the time of writing, Stella's Instagram followers have dropped to just over 27,000, eight years after the debut of HFM, and her bio now states 'Minjoon & Jei's mom'. Instead, she is slowly reverting to documenting her family life for their personal enjoyment, and expresses gratitude for the opportunities that the children once had thanks to their time on the reality show. Before we part, Stella tells me more about her day job, which involves fashion. I remark that this must be why her family is always well dressed on Instagram – she knows that I am a fan. To this, Stella reveals in half-jest that her long-standing request to her family till this day is that they coordinate their outfits when they go on outings on weekends, to look presentable and coherent, both in person and in the photographs.

As I leave the interview and board the Seoul Metropolitan Subway to head to my next interview, I scroll through Stella's Instagram account once more, and note photographs of the family in 'Osoroi Code' – the Japanese practice of families or friends dressing similarly when they go out to demonstrate homophily. I bookmarked a post of Stella and her husband clad in black and white, and the children in pink and white, and another post of the family dressed in green and white blocks and stripes. Stella's honest accounting of her children's journey from TV fame, to social media fandom, to family Influencer celebrity, and the return to 'normalcy' was refreshing. I mused in my fieldnotes that while the afterlives of reality TV fame for some children have been very damaging, in this instance, the children have emerged with (the mild inconvenience of) a coordinated fashion sense, thanks to a farsighted and fashionable mom.

Conclusion

In general, children who are involved in variety show celebrity have opted into the production, whether via the proxy of their guardians for the younger children, or by themselves as teenagers. Their online fame ranges from local to international markets, resulting in transient to long-term opportunities, where their personal brand and identities may be unknown or solidly anchored. While the opportunities for monetization and in-routes into other more stable forms of online celebrity, like family Influencers (see chapter 3) or viral stars (see chapter 7), might differ, it is important to note that these children have at least some awareness of their initial springboard into internet fame. In the next chapter, we continue our insights on the Korean entertainment industry by considering how the mainstream music industry and social media industry work together as 'factories' to cultivate international child celebrities across domains and platforms.

9

Factories

Introduction

There are precedents for the 'factory-like' models that systematically groom child celebrity through routinized infrastructure and training: Disney's Mickey Mouse Club in the US and the *jimusho* idol training system in Japan (Lee et al. 2024: 5) are world-renowned examples. We were previously introduced to the model of spotting and grooming viral child stars into mainstream child celebrity adopted by *The Ellen DeGeneres Show* (chapter 7). Pivoting to the Korean market, we also previously considered several prolific case studies of children who are active in the variety show productions in Korea (chapter 8). In this chapter, we consider some of the scaffolding and infrastructure that has developed around the talent management of child Influencers and other 'internet famous' children online. We then look at a lengthier case study of how one such child star, the multi-hyphenate Ella Gross, has already by age sixteen cycled through the circuits of internet celebrity, child models, K-pop networks, child Influencers, K-pop trainees and, most recently, K-pop idols.

Talent Management

Throughout my body of work on Influencer cultures, I have detailed the structure and workings of Influencer agencies, talent incubators and managerial intermediaries in several accounts and across many settings (e.g. Abidin 2017b, 2018). In brief, *Influencer managers* are the backend professionals who work the most closely with Influencers. They broker the client and brand offers for the Influencer, manage their schedule of in-person appearances and social media programming, strategize and oversee their content production, supervise follower sentiment, mediate press requests and appearances, craft PR and publicity campaigns, mitigate bad press and publicity, and even balance the accounts books. In one of my earlier stints of fieldwork for my PhD and later for my postdoc, I worked as an Influencer manager on occasions and shadowed several managers from different companies on several assignments. In reality and in all honesty, I find Influencer managers to be multi-talented and multi-functional 'Swiss Army knives' akin to highly professional personal assistants. I have observed up close and first hand Influencer managers who manage house keys and pets and plants when their talents are on holiday; those who when accompanying their Influencers on overseas assignments are responsible for the minutiae down to packing of luggage; and those who have laughed and cried alongside their Influencers amidst professional and personal milestones. For Influencers who are more established, managers are often the first responders, the first port of call, the first gatekeepers of access.

While some Influencer managers are freelancers or run their own one-person companies, many work for *Influencer or talent agencies* who aggregate and represent a collection of Influencers to potential clients, and provide a wide suite of services to Influencers to manage every aspect of their business. Historically, the scholarship on Influencers on video platforms like YouTube refers to such agencies as *multi-channel networks* (MCN), and in specific markets like China, MCNs are equivalent to Influencer agencies given the very broad range of in-house services that they provide. The more established and larger of these companies may have dedicated staff members to oversee the specific roles usually taken on by the 'Swiss Army knife' managers – such as accountants, PR liaisons, risk mitigation teams, lawyers, personal assistants and the like – so that the managers can focus their work on maintaining the welfare and wellbeing of the Influencers.

Many companies also have dedicated *production crews* who assist with producing, editing and scheduling Influencer contents, whether in their in-house studios or off-site. This level of professionalism is quite unlike the early wave of Influencers who used to 'DIY' every aspect of their content production and their business. Influencer agencies also have in-house units or subsidiaries focused specifically on being *talent incubators.* These focus on scouting fresh faces and budding talents, and training them to be ready for the Influencer market. It is not uncommon for agencies and incubators to also run *creator academies* that design and provide (usually paid) courses for aspirants to learn the very many skills needed to navigate the Influencer industry.

The Multi-Hyphenate Ella Gross

Ella Gross was born in 2008 to an American father and a Korean mother, and has since childhood spent her time between California, where her family lives, and Seoul, where she has worked since she was a child. At two-years-old, she starred in her first print ads and experienced waves of virality over the years for her beautiful facial features. At eight-years-old, she experienced a major wave of virality and became internationally prominent for her mixed-race background, as she began to represent both American and Korean brands in the global market. At age ten, it was announced that Gross had formally signed with The Black Label, a recording label which is a subsidiary of YG Entertainment, which in turn is one of the top three K-pop entertainment agencies in the world. Since then, she has been widely anticipated to be 'the face' of the 'next generation' of K-pop idols for the 'international market'. In 2024, just before she turned sixteen, Gross debuted with K-pop idol girl group Meovv under the helm of world renowned K-pop producer Teddy Park.

Internet celebrity

I first commenced digital ethnography on Ella Gross's online profiles in 2017, after I came across her Instagram account on my feed during another one of her waves of virality. I instantly recognized Gross as the 'baby model' whom I had often seen on Instagram and Tumblr fan accounts as she had a distinct mixed-race appearance. My fieldnotes document Instagram photos of Gross showing off the new Vans sneakers she had recently acquired, demonstrating social consciousness as she masked up while heading outdoors, being made up for professional photoshoots, sitting in the backseat of a car en route to school, having dinner with her family at various eateries, strutting down yet another cat walk. As a follower, the scrolling experience often solicited whiplash, but Gross always seemed to be elegantly transitioning between the glitz and glamour of high fashion and luxury, and the mundane minutiae of life as a nine-year-old burdened with school homework. Of course, this persona was aimed at communicating relatability with followers (see chapter 3), and finely curated by the person behind the camera and Instagram account: Gross's mother.

At the time of my first data collection, Gross had 1.6 million followers on Instagram across 882 posts. Her bio indicated that her account was 'Run by Mom'. It was clear that even early into her role as an internet celebrity, Gross's mother was already visible and established as an intermediary, a buffer, a safeguard for her daughter's interfaces and interactions with the public. She often responded to select fan comments on Gross's behalf, would organize for Gross to respond to some fan Q&As on Instagram Stories, and has also been speculated by fan forums to moderate Gross's social media presence by deleting or muting haters and their comments. The structure of Gross's rise to fame on the internet here is akin to that of family Influencers (chapter 3) and child Influencers (chapter 4), where parasocial communications and strategic disclosure are especially important for maintaining a strong following. An example of an exchange between Gross's fandom and her mother-as-Instagram-manager is as follows:

> Fan account: Hi, I would like to know if you (Ella's mom) is ok with fan accounts, me and other fan accounts want to hear your thoughts because you might be uncomfortable with them! Please answer [*sic*]
>
> Mother: of course we appreciate all of Ella's fans :) thank you!

Mid-way through my data collection in 2019, the Gross Instagram account boasted over 3.6 million followers. At the time of writing, her account has 4.2 million followers, but all her posts and her biography have been deleted, following her debut with Meovv (see below). However, like many other 'internet famous' children (see chapters 6 and 8), there are thousands of fan-managed repositories that have archived all her past social media posts, and that continue to curate updates on Gross's media appearances and sightings in public.

Child model

Alongside her internet celebrity, Ella Gross was professionally known as a child model in the fashion industry. In fact, even at the time of her debut with Meovv in 2024, news reports would refer to her as 'former child model' and 'child Influencer'. At the time of writing, Gross's modelling contracts appear to be negotiated through her record label company. But in the earlier years when she was managed by modelling agencies, her continued ascension to childhood fame was carefully orchestrated through the machinery of boutique talent scouts, luxury brand liaisons and high fashion PR staff. She has regular features in prolific magazines, opportunities to star in print and digital advertisements, and also makes appearances at events.

However, in addition to the 'factory' of child modelling, Gross's Instagram often also tapped into her fellow child model network as cultural capital. These include photographs of Gross and other world-famous child models spending time together, either in professional settings such as backstage selfies or during meal breaks while filming, or in casual settings such as hanging out at a fast-food joint or sitting together at a table to complete their homework. These Instagram posts would often usher fans of other child models to Gross's account, and the mutual exposure across fandoms from tagging both models' social media handles facilitated the expansion of their Instagram following and fan base.

One fellow child model who appeared frequently in Gross's contents was Russian child model Kristina Pimenova, who was three years older than Gross. Fans would often point out similarities between Gross and Pimenova, or sleuth into the veracity of their 'offline' friendship. On one occasion, Gross uploaded a photograph of herself clad in a pink military blazer with elaborate embroidered rope – a distinctive fashion article, so to speak. Hawk-eyed fans were quick to spot a connection between Gross and Pimenova:

> Fan account: Why i sometimes see ella's wore the same clothes that kristina wore in the past ? I mean not in this picture, btw I love the jacket, where did she get it from ? [*sic*]

> Fan account: yeah me too. Maybe kristina gave her some old clothes or they match sometimes?? [*sic*]

Multiple threads on the Instagram post speculated whether Gross and Pimenova had the same fashion taste, whether they were gifted the same item, whether they were besties who purchased the same jacket, or whether Gross was simply 'copying' Pimenova's dress sense. To this, Gross's mother takes control of the rumour mongering and responds in a masterclass of a comment that paints both girls in a good light: 'Ella is so lucky! Kristina gives Ella clothes she's grown out of. They're like sisters ♥'

K-pop networker

Just as I found Gross's face familiar when she reappeared on my Instagram feed some years after I was already accustomed to seeing her likeness on various social media, K-pop fans will no doubt be familiar with Gross as she began to regularly appear on the social media contents of the BLACKPINK members. To give brief context for the unacquainted: BLACKPINK is a YG Entertainment pop idol girl group formed in 2016, comprising Jennie, Jisoo, Lisa and Rosé. Collectively, the women have cultural roots and backgrounds in Australia, Korea, New Zealand and Thailand, and are one of the most successful, record-breaking female K-pop acts of all time. As such, Gross's appearance on their personal Instagram accounts is no minor matter, as she is literally platformed, spotlighted and promoted to hundreds of millions of eyeballs worldwide; at the time of writing, the BLACKPINK members boast over 354 million followers across their four personal Instagram accounts. It is no wonder that Gross became swiftly branded as 'BLACKPINK's baby' or 'baby Jennie' – owing to her likeness to the rapper – by fans around the globe.

Figure 9.1. Artist impression of K-pop trainee Ella Gross in a viral photograph with BLACKPINK when she was a child, and a newer photograph when she regrouped with them as a teen K-pop star.

It is at this stage that Gross appeared to leverage the narratives of K-pop sistership and mentee networking as social capital. She experienced a halo effect via her physical and digital proximity to BLACKPINK, and was now widely discussed across both K-pop fandom and child modelling forums (Lee and Abidin 2023). Gross's prominence in K-pop networks is in part also because she appears to have a sustained and ongoing relationship with the women of BLACKPINK, such that their mentions and tags of her are not perceived as paid promotions or sponsored contents in the first instance. Gross's Instagram documents several photographs of her spending time with the women over months and years, in various cities around the world.

There are photographs of Gross standing among the BLACKPINK women and being embraced in a group hug; photographs of Gross comfortably leaning into a large couch surrounded by the BLACKPINK stars; photographs of Gross raised up between the BLACKPINK members at the backstage of their concert. There is a post of Gross and Jennie giving the same wink in response to a fan commentary that they are 'mother and daughter'; a post of Gross holding up a product she spotted in a store that features Jennie as the ambassador and model; a post of Gross sharing a cosy meal with Rosé; a post of Gross and Rosé operating a jukebox at a bar; a post of Gross and Jisoo playing a hand clapping game. On these posts, the women of BLACKPINK would often leave comments or emojis fawning over Gross.

In the K-pop networking era, Gross borrowed from the register of K-pop collaborations and social media intimacy to establish herself in the industry, gaining a footing in yet another sector. Her fame from internet celebrity and child modelling appeared to seamlessly cross over into the mainstream entertainment industry, as even Korean and Japanese actors, singers and models began to post photographs together with her on their personal Instagram accounts. She was 'the celebrity sighting' that was most coveted, and by celebrities themselves no less.

Child Influencer

Throughout the child modelling and K-pop networking stages of Gross's career, she continued to maintain her activities as a child Influencer. The management of this variety of fame has been discussed earlier in the book (see chapter 4), but here I spotlight how Gross's mother appears to manage backlash in moments of controversy. As my earlier accounts note, there has been every effort made on Gross's Instagram to produce the impression that despite being a world-famous internet celebrity and child model, she has a balanced and normal childhood involving the mundanities of school and family life. Her mother also skilfully relies on the goodwill – and voluntary labour – of fans to extend the discourse that Gross is 'just a regular child'. In her curation of Q&As from fans, Gross's mother appears to spotlight queries that remind the public that she is a child, focusing on age-appropriate hobbies and interests like 'Who's your fav Disney princess?' Other questions that stream in during her Instagram Live that focus on the more adult aspects of her work – like how much she is paid for a campaign or what her training hours are like – literally fly past the screen as thousands of in-streaming comments from thousands of live fans move the conversation along quickly.

However, despite her very successful parenting in facilitating Gross's career from babyhood to teenhood, this journey has not been without criticism. Gross's mother has been called out for lacking responsibility as a parent for 'overworking' Gross; fans claim she is 'exploitative' in her constant references to BLACKPINK to leverage their celebrity; and she was accused of 'sexualizing a minor' when Gross starred in a Baskin-Robbins television commercial that appeared to draw on suggestive innuendos (Lee and Abidin 2023). Direct responses to these claims were not sighted on Gross's Instagram account during my digital ethnography. But there were other instances where rumour-mongering that originated in fan forums (see chapter 10) was indirectly addressed through the strategic publishing of select contents on Instagram.

For instance, in response to accusations that Gross has undergone plastic surgery or that she constantly dyes her hair dark (fans have spotted that Gross's younger brother Roman is blonde) to 'Asian-fish' and appeal to the Asian market, her Instagram features an old family photograph of her blonde

American dad, her brunette Korean mom, a brunette young Gross and a blonde young brother Roman. The playful caption reads: '#throwbackthursday Ella, age 4 [emoji of a girl with black hair] Roman, age 2 [emoji of a boy with blond hair] Daddy and Mommy age undisclosed'. Fans have noted the subtle responses by Gross's mother, and subsequently screengrabs of these posts and her captions have been reposted by fans as an 'unofficial defence' in the very forums that initiated the rumour-mongering.

K-pop trainee

In 2018, it was announced that Gross had signed an exclusive contract with The Black Label. While the news took the industry by storm and appeared in multiple headlines, fans had long anticipated this announcement since the early days of her public K-pop networking; the announcement merely confirmed their speculations. News coverage pivoted slightly away from the usual fixations on Gross's mixed-race beauty, to focus on how she was going to be the 'visuals' of her K-pop group – K-pop lingo referring to the most attractive member in the pop group, usually the face of the group (Lee and Abidin 2023). The media machinery of the K-pop industry was hard at work, churning out articles pitting Gross as 'the next Jennie' (of BLACKPINK), and positing that her K-pop idol group was going to be 'the little sister' of BLACKPINK.

Just as Gross was parachuted into mainstream celebrity and attention via her affiliation with YG Entertainment and BLACKPINK, the company and idol group also benefited from these associations as they were perceived to be 'family-like', 'family-friendly' and 'globally' competitive, given Gross's unique ties with Korea and the US (Lee and Abidin 2023). In prior work, digital media scholar Jin Lee and I (Lee and Abidin 2023) highlighted how this partnership was an exemplar of 'co-branding', or a 'strategic alliance that connects two or more brands in the marketplace' (Askegaard and Bengtsson 2005 cited in Lee and Abidin 2023: 81). Elsewhere, I have discussed the operations of K-pop training facilities and their early promotions of 'popular' or 'famous' trainees (Lee et al. 2024) – that is, trainees who have already accumulated a significant fan base and public brand image despite not yet having formally debuted in a group. This is a common occurrence for trainees of the 'Big Three' K-pop companies – JYP Entertainment, SM Entertainment and YG Entertainment – who often train for years but debut into an already-available, already-informed, already-ready fan base. Here, I continue to highlight the strategic use of social media to house and streamline Gross's childhood fame.

After the announcement, subsequent posts of Gross show her in The Black Label studio, although the pictures are often framed in angles (e.g. important details or identities of people obscured) and overlaid with aesthetics (e.g. blurred effect, desaturation of colour) that are intentionally ambiguous to bait attention and stimulate speculative conversation. In one post, Gross is seen in the setting of a studio, occupying most of the foreground. In the background, we see the back of a man managing a soundboard, likely a sound engineer or a music producer. His face is obscured, but fans gather from his height, build and the fashion sense conveyed through his pairing of a cap with a baggy printed hoodie with baggy jeans that he must be the world-renowned K-pop producer Teddy Park. There are rumours that Gross is already recording in the studio despite her only recently signing with the label, and other rumours that she is sitting in on senior colleagues' recordings to learn and be mentored. Regardless, the aim of the Instagram post has been achieved: to stimulate interest, create anticipation, and pave new pathways for fans to track Gross's journey as a K-pop trainee through this new series of breadcrumbs.

K-pop idol

As I mentioned above, at the time of writing Gross has debuted in Meovv, a five-piece K-pop idol girl group composed of Anna, Ella, Gawon, Narin and Sooin. The girls are young, aged between sixteen- and nineteen-years-old, with Ella Gross being the youngest. Collectively, they have cultural and birth roots in Japan, Korea and the US, and – like BLACKPINK – have been marketed to appeal to a global market. Gross has now truly entered the height of all celebrity 'factory' systems, as an active performer in the K-pop idol industry. Even as she grows out of being a 'child celebrity', she continues to be a bona fide celebrity, and a veteran one at that, who has transversed multiple star systems and factories. By late-2024, Meovv has released three singles and won awards for being 'Rising Artists' in the K-pop industry.

Conclusion

This chapter has considered the different systems of child (internet) celebrity management with which child Influencers may find themselves entangled. We are in a climate where the child Influencer industry is becoming increasingly professionalized, which is attractive to many aspirants who perceive it to be a career with systematic in-routes and pathways to success. The case studies throughout the book and the backend stakeholders detailed above evidence this. At the same time, child celebrities in the mainstream entertainment industries are also placing a foot in the child Influencer factory, as modelling agencies and actor managers require auditionees to have already-established social media profiles, personal brands and followings as criteria to qualify for casting calls. In the next chapter, we consider the very critical role of followers, fans and anti-fans/haters, who are important mediators for escalating issues and concerns surrounding 'internet famous' children through networks of fora and social media collectively known as 'Ground Zero'.

10

Ground Zero

Introduction

I was raised by a military father and in my upbringing 'Ground Zero' was parlance in our everyday conversation from as early as I can remember. Whenever we left home on adventures and excursions, the first thing my dad would do was to mark the beginning of our journey as 'Ground Zero', the starting base of our activity, the meeting point where we would agree to wait if we were ever separated in a crowd. Whenever we worked on puzzles and crafts and I had messed up, my dad would simply state that we would need to begin again from 'Ground Zero', from the very beginning, methodically from the start. But I also understood 'Ground Zero' in a literal sense, through years of being my dad's companion through way too many military movies: 'Ground Zero' was the site of disaster, the epicentre of a blast, the detonation point. For many 'internet famous' children who have been or will be embroiled in controversy at some point, 'Ground Zero' is all of the above, and specifically dispersed in networks of discussion forums, online chatter and comments sections.

Recent scholarship in the field of Influencer research has highlighted the importance of grassroots online communities and networks of followers to govern the Influencer industry, especially in instances or markets where formal government regulations and industry guidelines may still be lacking. A recent special issue of *Policy & Internet* journal on 'Influencer Regulations, Governance, and Socio-cultural Issues in Asia' (Abidin et al. 2023) presents several examples of such governance from the ground, whether via the 'vernacular' governance of Influencers who commit racist faux pas in Singapore (Radics and Abidin 2022), or the 'soft' regulation of foreign-national Influencers who venture into nationalist discourse on South Korean YouTube (Lee and Abidin 2022). In this vein, child Influencers and their 'internet famous' companions have similarly been subject to governance from the ground through platforms like Reddit and a plethora of pseudonymous online fora. These spaces are often the detonation points where watchful followers debut conversations and concern around the wellbeing of 'internet famous' children, leading to extended and nuanced networks of discourse that quickly proliferate across platforms and the mainstream media. Indeed, mainstream media coverage of 'internet famous' children often point to such 'Ground Zero' as repositories of evidence, or simply lift screengrabs from the links arduously curated by these anonymous vigilantes.

But lest we misconceive 'Ground Zero' as a caustic hotbed of ridicule and hatred, take heart that 'Ground Zero' in the context of 'internet famous' children is almost always governed by literal 'community guidelines'. My digital ethnography of such online fora in multiple East Asian languages and the dozens of dedicated subreddits in the English language often display 'bible-like' commandments in the 'About' tab, setting the boundaries of permissible discourse. Typical rules usually set limits on the types of content permitted on the thread, the nature of conversation permitted, the forms of 'evidence' that can be offered, an agreement not to 'dox' or over-expose minors and vulnerable others, strict prohibitions on making 'direct contact' with the Influencers being discussed, and

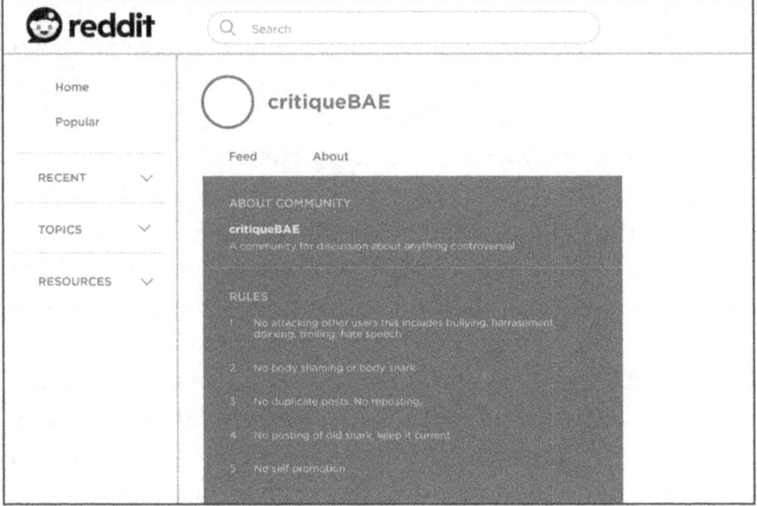

Figure 10.1. Artist impression of an example of 'snark forums' on Reddit, displaying the typical rules governing the online community.

general mores and norms regarding the use of civil language. In some fora, the threads specify the nature of the discourse and the agenda of the conversation allowed, simply stating whether they are 'fan threads', 'hate threads', 'for speculation' or for specific causes like 'saving' a child victim or 'collecting evidence' of child abuse.

Such practices can be understood as 'lateral surveillance' or 'peer monitoring', and involve individuals 'adopting practices associated with marketing and law enforcement to gain information about' others (Andrejevic 2002: 479). Originally nestled in studies of police history and state surveillance (Reeves 2012), later iterations of lateral surveillance have evolved to take place online as 'social media surveillance' (Trottier and Lyon 2011) or 'online surveillance' that can permeate the 'economic', 'political' and 'cultural' aspects of everyday life (Fuchs 2015).

Community Governance

In recent work, sociologist Alex Turvy and I (Turvy and Abidin 2025) propose that community governance of 'internet famous' children emerges in more-or-less standardized ways. Following the early legacies of scholarship that framed discourse on feminist blogs as 'discursive activism online' (Shaw 2012) that required 'emotional investments' (Shaw 2013), the advocacy work of 'Ground Zero' workers relies on the 'digital gossip economy' (Rauchberg and Maddox 2024). Below, I describe the framework of 'community governance' through four steps: gossip-milling, rumour-mongering, trash-talking and calling-out. The cycle usually involves enthusiastic followers spotting something amiss in a post, initiating conversations in the comment sections to invite other users to chime in, and co-establishing the acceptable boundaries for parent-and-child content online through networked discourse.

Gossip-milling: Gossip-milling begins as informal chatter among followers whose keen observations of online posts form the source contents for others to partake in the conversation. Gossip instigators often experience 'status enhancement' (see Farley 2019) for their leadership in disrupting the status quo and power of influencers. Given the varying reliability of gossip, rumour-mongering emerges when followers read accounts with interest and spread the hearsay widely.

Rumour-mongering: Rumour-mongering is the vernacular practice that usually ignites a network of informal community governance, allowing the usually voiceless 'subordinates' to assert some agency (see Coast and Fox 2015). This aligns with broader observations about influencer gossip cultures, where follower-led investigations often fuel public accountability mechanisms (Lawson 2024). Rumour-mongering also extends mainstream interest in controversies surrounding 'internet famous children' beyond the comment sections of a post, as the conversation becomes supplemented by follower reports and chatter in related threads across various fora like Reddit and local parenting webpages. It is not uncommon for this discourse to also inform tabloids and popular news reports, amplifying controversies in ways that shape influencer reputations and public scrutiny (Abidin 2023).

Trash-talking: When an issue has accrued mainstream publicity via tabloids and news discourse, pedestrians from outside the subculture are likely to chime in through trash-talking, where disrespectful insults are openly cast on the parent who has posted the TikTok video, for example, in the spirit of rivalry between different TikTok subcultures (see Yip et al. 2018). At this stage, the discourse by commentators is often shrouded in moral judgements and implicitly carries arrogance and condescension towards the KidTok community at large, in part due to their unfamiliarity with the subculture. This mirrors broader trends in influencer scrutiny, where follower gossip and call-outs play a significant role in regulating perceived transgressions, particularly around financial disclosures and ethical conduct (Lee and Abidin 2021).

Calling-out: Following this, users are often spurred by the spike in attention on their community to hold each other accountable, and continue with calling-out by asking the parent who has posted the wrongful contents to explain their actions, acknowledge their wrong, and seek redress through an apology to the community and a declaration to correct their behaviours to match the yardsticks co-fashioned by the discursive network (see Lawson 2020).

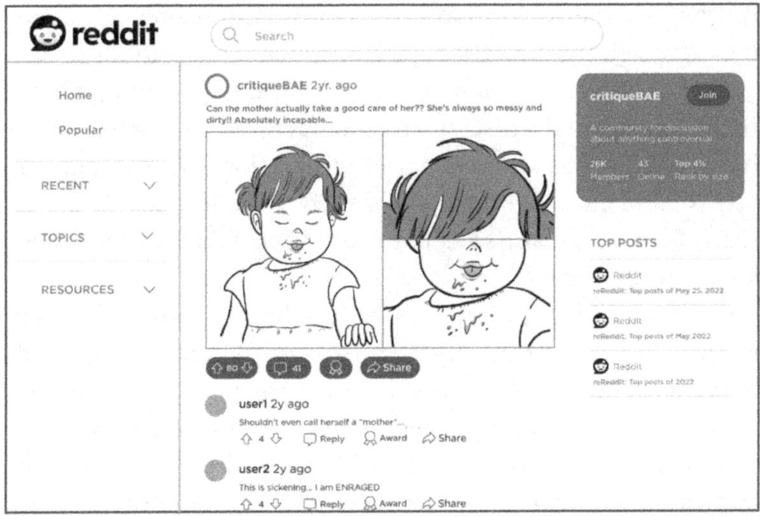

Figure 10.2. Artist impression of an example of a 'trash talk' post on Reddit, featuring zoomed in screenshots of children who are allegedly mistreated or not well taken care of.

The 'Wren Eleanor' Scandal

Wren Eleanor, a Nebraska-based toddler, and her mother Jacquelyn rose to KidTok (see chapter 5) fame with over 17 million followers at their peak. Wren, born in 2019, appeared in daily lifestyle vlogs, gaining viral attention through song covers and cute moments. However, in 2022, when Wren was three, followers began scrutinizing alarming patterns in the posts, initiating community governance.

Gossip-milling

Followers raised concerns about videos showing Wren in bathing suits and engaging in questionable activities mimicking adult behaviours, such as pretending to use makeup, deodorant and a razor on her genitals in a 'get ready with me' (GRWM) routine, playing with a tampon, and 'breastfeeding' a stuffed toy. Although these might appear as innocent imitations of her mother, followers pointed out during the gossip-milling phase that Jacquelyn had a history of sexualizing Wren. For example, the 'breastfeeding' video featured the caption 'Just feeding her kitty ♥' and hashtags like '#breastfed #toddler #sweet #fyp', which followers claimed decontextualized Wren's roleplay to boost engagement.

In another post, Wren is seen holding a bottle of honey between her legs, struggling to squeeze out a tube of semi-solid honey with her hands tightly grasping the neck of the bottle. Each time the honey emerges, Wren bends down to suck it, giggling and chirping, 'it's sticky!' Followers pointed out that Wren's positioning and reactions could be decontextualized as fellatio. Similarly, a video of Wren eating a spicy pickle, featuring close-up shots of her smacking lips, licking, making slobbery noises and grunting with satisfaction – all without any commentary or interaction from Jacquelyn – raised concerns about the framing and focus as being intentionally sexualized.

Rumour-mongering

As hundreds of thousands of comments flooded Wren's TikToks, parenting fora and Reddit threads, community governance kicked into high gear. In-depth discussions debated whether these were innocuous childhood moments or something more troubling, with followers emphasizing Jacquelyn's lack of response to their concerns. During this rumour-mongering phase, conspiracy theories proliferated as followers noticed Jacquelyn engaging with positive comments while appearing to ignore criticism. Wren's account went increasingly viral as invested KidTok community members, TikTokers and YouTubers curated and commented on her suggestive content. A dedicated Reddit sub, created in April

2022 and amassing over 25,000 followers, clearly conveyed the community's stance, stating,

> This is not a fan sub. A place to discuss the child exploitation of Wren Eleanor from TikTok.

The collaborative efforts of the KidTok community exposed deeply troubling interactions, including adult men creating duets simulating masturbation, smacking their lips and posting sexualized captions. Followers shared evidence of adult male accounts exclusively following young girls, consistently saving Wren's content, and frequently commenting on her posts. Even more alarming was the discovery of fan accounts reposting Wren's content with overtly sexualized framing. The community's concerns gained legitimacy when high-profile members like self-identified 'former FBI special agent' TikToker Tracy Walder shared expert perspectives on how law enforcement would view the content (Bilal 2024). As mainstream media coverage intensified, it amplified both Wren's virality and the skilled investigative work of KidTok followers, such as exposing the disturbing digital footprints and suggestive usernames of frequent commenters (Bilal 2024).

Trash-talking

As the scandal persisted without a response from Jacquelyn to followers or press inquiries (Dickson 2022; Kindelan 2022), the trash-talking phase erupted. Tens of thousands of commentators, including opportunistic creators seeking to capitalize on the viral controversy, openly criticized Jacquelyn. Using hashtags like '#controversy', '#drama', '#spillthetea' and '#viral', some creators amplified the issue to millions (e.g. @iNabber 2024). TikTok and YouTube commentary employed sensationalized headlines to drive engagement, such as:

> KidToker Exploiting Her Child For Predators
> The world's worst mother on TikTok
> Wren Eleanor's mother is under fire. . . AGAIN!
> Young mother RUINING her child's life
> Revealing the disturbing reality about Wren's mother

Dedicated threads on fora that were trash-talking Jacquelyn and Wren used similar attention-grabbing titles:

> OH MY GOD
> This makes me so sick
> I can't believe this is still happening

Calling-out

Owing to Jacquelyn's long-term silence on the matter, the *calling-out* phase appeared to turn towards targeting law enforcement agencies and the TikTok platform. Community members were urging each other to continue reporting Wren's TikTok posts for violating community guidelines, and would continually update each other on the progress on Reddit and other fora:

> I've already reported her posts several times but TikTok just responds that the content doesn't violate Community Guidelines
> Here is more Wren evidence, for those of you who want to flag older posts for CG violation.

Even though there were also several threads evidencing efforts to coordinate mass reporting, followers were frustrated that the platform did not consider their concerns seriously. When contacted for comment by a mainstream news outlet, a TikTok spokesperson indicated that they 'cannot comment on a specific account' and pointed to in-app features for protecting user safety, including Family Pairing features of minors, limiting comments and downloads, and that the platform will remove content that violates community guidelines like a video that 'depicts or promotes physical abuse, neglect, endangerment, or psychological disparagement of minors' (Kindelan 2022). However, this gap in the guidelines assigns responsibility and due diligence to the guardian of KidTok accounts, and ultimately does not address issues when the guardian is the very parent engaging in questionable practices. Followers then escalated their efforts by appealing to law enforcement, with long discussions on threads like:

> Why is the government not doing anything? Here is a list of authorities whom you can contact.
> This is no longer snark, this is legal evidence. Let's continue our efforts.
> Sign this petition to save Wren!!!

In August 2022, Jacquelyn finally responded with a TikTok post widely branded by followers as the 'apology video'. In it, she explains that posting snippets of Wren began as a 'hobby' and 'digital scrap book' to contain memories of her journey as a single parent. She also asserts:

> Wren is my number one priority, and her upbringing and safety are my top job, 24 hours a day . . .
>
> . . . This account has allowed me to provide for my daughter and to set aside money for the future. I'm not sure how this conspiracy theory got started and spiralled out of control. What you need to know is that no law enforcement agencies I conferred with – including the FBI – have found any proof that my daughter's likeness appears on inappropriate websites . . .

The Aftermath of Community Governance

Despite the apology, the cycle of *gossip-milling, rumour-mongering, trash-talking and calling-out* persisted. Followers accused Jacquelyn of the wilful ignorance about child predators, of the continued publication of Wren in compromising positions, and pointed to ongoing evidence of Wren's image being decontextualized and sexualized on other platforms.

Following 'the apology', Jacquelyn's continued posting of similar content drew mixed reactions. One news article (Dickson 2022) noted

> To be clear, there is no evidence that Jacquelyn is exploiting Wren in any way. Rather, the concern seems to be centered more on the type of content Jacquelyn is posting.

However, numerous articles highlighted the Wren Eleanor controversy's domino effect, raising the standards of community governance on KidTok and prompting parents to re-evaluate their social media practices. This evidenced that the efforts of community governance culminated in a thoughtful pause as parents were aware of the mom-shaming that Jacquelyn and other parents who exploit child Influencers experienced, but also understand the value of some social media posting to curate memories or potentially earn a healthy income as stay-at-home parents (Organ 2022). Ultimately, the prevailing sentiment was that the controversy sparked a crucial conversation about the risks of sharing children's content online, regardless of intent (Dickson 2022). Headlines captured this complex discourse:

> 'A toddler on TikTok is spawning a massive mom-led movement' in *RollingStone* (Dickson 2022)
> 'Parents remove videos of their kids from TikTok after "Wren Eleanor" warning' in *ABC News* (Kindelan 2022)

> 'Why the Wren Eleanor controversy makes parents so uncomfortable' in *Motherly* (Organ 2022)

In July 2024, Wren Eleanor's TikTok account suddenly appeared to be 'wiped', with all posts deleted and the bio removed. At the time of writing, the follower count has dropped from 17 million to 16.6 million, and the account retains over 622 million likes and still features the profile picture of Wren and Jacquelyn. While there were minor celebrations on various fora, the community governance efforts of the KidTok community have not stopped. Many threads and fora previously dedicated to Wren have since focused on other children across platforms who recently emerged and who appear to be in a similar plight:

> Is this Wren Eleanor 2.0?
> This is Wren all over again.
> Next gen Wren

Through the Wren Eleanor case study, the arduous labour by KidTok followers demonstrates their investment in holding prolific KidTok creators responsible, and in their pursuit of 'truths' to reaffirm community norms and thresholds for acceptable behaviour in the community.

Conclusion

Evidently, 'Ground Zero' can be fertile ground for productive conversation and governance by the grassroots, but there are also instances when the chatter becomes conspiracy theory that goes 'too far' and becomes harmful (see chapter 5). Yet, in other contexts, participants in 'Ground Zero' may become enticed by the allure of the very internet celebrity they are dissecting, and focus more on their own status and visibility within their communities of governance. In my digital ethnography I

Figure 10.3. Artist impression of an example of popular posts on Korean discussion forums, where fans and haters are active commentators who at times compete for the most 'up-voted' comments.

observed instances of this occurring, especially on discussion platforms that prize the 'popularity' of individual comments through up- and down-votes, or emoticon flares.

Without naming and shaming specific platforms, such models of comment ranking are popular on various Korean forums, where initial conversations that first began as sincere call-outs quickly descend into vitriol and malice. This underscores the fine line between community governance and 'mobbing' or group bullying, which in turn underscores the importance of the establishing and committing to the ground rules of 'Ground Zero'.

Conclusion

The subtitle of this book points to the complex and complicated nature by which we conceptualize and define 'Child Influencers', as it involves a myriad of ways for 'how children become entangled with social media fame'. While convenient to deploy in speech as a shorthand, using the blanket term 'child influencers' to refer to all types of 'internet famous' children obscures the reality of their different working conditions, the different industry structures that groom them, the different regulations and guidelines available to them, and who is assigned responsibility for their wellbeing. Further, newer neologisms are emerging by the day – e.g. Kidfluencer, KidTuber, KidToker – which further obscure the important theorization and conceptualization of 'Child Influencers' based in different origin stories and histories.

In this sense, vocabulary is – quite literally – everything. Whether an agency deems a child in their roster as an 'Influencer' or a 'talent'; whether a brand deems a child in their branding a collateral, a 'hire' or a 'plus one'; whether a platform deems a child on their platform a 'user' or a 'creator'; whether the public views a child in a viral video or meme a 'celebrity' or 'ordinary child' – these have implications as to how we frame the conversation around the proximity of the child to the commercialism of the social media industry, and whether guidelines and policies from different regulators may apply to the child.

For example, when defined and perceived as 'Creators', children are often subject only to the community guidelines of platforms and their rules that govern the monetization of content. Beyond regulating the types of content that are allowable on their interface, platforms have very little oversight, control and jurisdiction over child creators and what happens before their content is actually uploaded to the site. This places the care of minors under the responsibility of their 'guardians' rather than the platforms. But when perceived as 'Influencers', some of the legacy and emergent legal frameworks, governance structures and areas of governance become more widely applicable to children, who are then subject to a wider array of guidelines, safeguards and protection.

In other words, this book has taken a deep dive into the varieties and neglected nuances of 'internet famous' children who have often been grouped under the umbrella of 'Child Influencers' because there is conceptual, theoretical and pragmatic utility in doing so. And this is increasingly important in light of emergent trends and changes in the social media landscape.

Media scholar Sonia Livingstone (2018: 170) reminds us that in the *age of datafication*, media studies need to consider the 'growing power of social media platforms and their innovative datafication processes' and also 'recogniz[e] rather than eras[e] audiences' relation to both the everyday lifeworld and the public world of citizen action, regulatory intervention, and the wider society'.

As platforms are increasingly savvy and sophisticated with their *fast-evolving features and affordances*, we need to investigate the spillover pressures of algorithmic visibility and negotiation (e.g. Cotter 2018) while also recognizing their potential for cultivating children's media literacies on their own terms (Lange 2014) as forms of 'techno-literacy practices' through 'multimodal textual competencies and semiotic choices' (Marsh 2004: 51).

The *proliferation of child-centred and child-created contents* underscores the need to develop frameworks of ethics and care that similarly centre the child (e.g. Burroughs and Feller 2021), considering a fine balance between protecting their safety and maintaining their wellbeing, and maximizing their opportunities for personal development and self-actualization.

As more governments are considering the *regulation of child Influencers* within their domestic jurisdictions, it is pressing to acknowledge the role and positionality of the child in assessing how they may come under the purview of labour laws and other online protections (e.g. Verdoodt et al. 2020).

This book is written as a product of its time, where the commodification of childhood for contemporary entertainment (Hudders et al. 2024) has fast become mainstream and accepted, while very new advancements such as generative AI and the emergent phenomena of children embroiled in new forms of tech-abuse are on the horizon (Barassi 2025). It is hoped that as an account of the histories and origin stories, typologies and nuances, and pathways and pivots to the phenomenon of 'child Influencers', this book will provide a history of how we got here, provocations for how to think about proliferating trends, and a blueprint of how to forecast and mitigate the challenges to come.

References

Abetz, J. and J. Moore (2018). '"Welcome to the mommy wars, ladies": Making sense of the ideology of combative mothering in mommy blogs'. *Communication, Culture and Critique,* 11(2), 265–81. https://doi.org/10.1093/ccc/tcy008

Abidin, C. (2015). 'Micromicrocelebrity: Branding babies on the internet'. *M/C Journal,* 18(5). https://doi.org/10.5204/mcj.1022

Abidin, C. (2016). '"Aren't these just young, rich women doing vain things online?": Influencer selfies as subversive frivolity'. *Social Media + Society,* 2(2), 1–17. https://doi.org/10.1177/2056305116641342

Abidin, C. (2017a). '#familygoals: Family influencers, calibrated amateurism, and justifying young digital labor'. *Social Media + Society,* 3(2), 1–15. https://doi.org/10.1177/2056305117707191

Abidin, C. (2017b). 'Influencer extravaganza: A decade of commercial "lifestyle" microcelebrities in Singapore'. In L. Hjorth, H. Horst, G. Bell and A. Galloway (eds.), *Routledge Companion to Digital Ethnography.* Abingdon: Routledge, 158–68. https://www.routledge.com/The-Routledge-Companion-to-Digital-Ethnography/Hjorth-Horst-Galloway-Bell/p/book/9781138940918

Abidin, C. (2018). *Internet Celebrity: Understanding Fame Online.* Bingley: Emerald Publishing. https://www.emerald.com/insight/publication/doi/10.1108/9781787560765

Abidin, C. (2019). 'K-pop on Instagram between South Korea and North America'. *Korean Studies Association of Australasia (KSAA) 2019 Biennial Conference,* Perth, Australia, 4–6 December.

Abidin, C. (2021). 'Mapping internet celebrity on TikTok: Exploring attention economies and visibility labours'. *Cultural Science Journal,* 12(1), 77–103. https://doi.org/10.5334/csci.140

Abidin, C. (2022). 'It's corn! How the online viral "Corn Kid" is on a well-worn path to fame in the child influencer industry'. *The Conversation,* 14 September. https://theconversation.com/its-corn-how-the-online-viral-corn-kid-is-on-a-well-worn-path-to-fame-in-the-child-influencer-industry-189974

Abidin, C. (2023). 'Child influencers: How children have become entangled with social media commerce'. *Australian Quarterly,* 94(3), 3–13. https://www.jstor.org/stable/e27221039

Abidin, C. (2025). *TikTok and Youth Cultures.* Bingley: Emerald Publishing.

Abidin, C., C. Gartland and K. Grant. (2025). 'TikTok & children: TikTok Cultures Research Network & TikTok Fireside Chat'. *International Journal of Cultural Studies* (online first). https:/doi.org/10.1177/13678779241307972

Abidin, C. and B.V. Kaye (2021). 'Audio memes, earworms, and templatability: The "aural turn" of memes on TikTok'. In C. Arkenbout, J. Wilson and D. de Zeeuw (eds.), *Critical Meme Reader: Global Mutations of the Viral Image.* Amsterdam: Institute of Network Cultures, 58–68. https://networkcultures.org/blog/publication/critical-meme-reader-global-mutations-of-the-viral-image/

Abidin, C. and J. Lee (2022). 'Social justice through social media pop cultures: Case studies and reading resources on influencers and TikTok'. TikTok Cultures Research Network (TCRN) & Social Media Pop Cultures Programme, Centre for Culture and Technology (CCAT), Curtin University. https://tiktokcultures.com/socialjustice2022/

Abidin, C. and J. Lee (2023). 'K-pop TikTok: TikTok's expansion into South Korea, TikTok Stage, and platformed glocalization'. *Media International Australia*, 188(1), 86–111. https://doi.org/10.1177/1329878X231186445

Abidin, C., J. Xu and J. Hutchinson (2023). 'Influencer regulations, governance and sociocultural issues in Asia'. *Policy & Internet*, 15(2), 340–57. https://doi.org/10.1002/poi3.340

Anderson, G., J.G. Moore and M. Vandenbeld Giles (2014). '"Doing it all. . . and making it look easy!": Yummy mummies, mompreneurs and the North American neoliberal crises of the home'. In M. Vandenbeld Giles (ed.), *Mothering in the Age of Neoliberalism*. Ontario: Demeter Press, 95–116. https://dc.arcabc.ca/islandora/object/dc%3A42465

Andrejevic, M. (2002). 'The work of watching one another: Lateral surveillance, risk, and governance'. *Surveillance & Society*, 2(4), 479–97. https://doi.org/10.24908/ss.v2i4.3359

Arnold, B.L. and B. Martin (eds.) (2016). *Taking the Village Online: Mothers, Motherhood and Social Media*. Ontario: Demeter Press. https://demeterpress.org/books/taking-the-village-online-mothers-motherhood-and-social-media-edited-by-lorin-basden-arnold-and-bettyann-martin/

Askegaard, S. and A. Bengtsson (2005). 'When Hershey met Betty: Love, lust and co-branding'. *Journal of Product & Brand Management*, 14(5), 322–9. https://doi.org/10.1108/10610420510616359

Balanzategui, J. (2021). '"Disturbing" children's YouTube genres and the algorithmic uncanny'. *New Media & Society*, 25(12), 3521–42. https://doi.org/10.1177/14614448211049264

Barassi, V. (2025). 'Amplified visibility: Critical reflections on children's social media presence, sharenting and tech-abuse in the age of generative AI'. In T. Annabell, C. Fieseler, C. Goanta and I. Wildhaber (eds.), *The Hashtag Hustle: Law and Policy Perspectives on Working in the Influencer Economy*. Cheltenham: Edward Elgar, 13–31. https://doi.org/10.4337/9781035332816

Beuckels, E. and R. De Wolf. (2024). 'Social media influencers as new agents on parenthood? A systematic literature review of parent influencer research and a future research agenda'. *Information, Communication & Society*, 28(4), 744–62. https://doi.org/10.1080/1369118X.2024.2334913

Bilal, K. (2024). 'Wren Eleanor: All you need to know about the controversial preschool TikTok star'. *Find My Kids*, 30 August. https://findmykids.org/blog/en/wren-eleanor-and-jacquelyn-controversy

Blanchet, B. (2022). '"Ellen DeGeneres Show" star Sophia Grace reveals she's pregnant'. *People Magazine*, 22 October. https://people.com/parents/ellen-sophia-grace-reveals-she-is-pregnant/

Blum-Ross, A. (2015). '"Sharenting": Parent bloggers and managing children's digital footprints'. *LSE Blog*, 17 June. https://blogs.lse.ac.uk/parenting4digitalfuture/2015/06/17/managing-your-childs-digital-footprint-and-or-parent-bloggers-ahead-of-brit-mums-on-the-20th-of-june/

Blum-Ross, A. and S. Livingstone (2017). '"Sharenting," parent blogging, and the boundaries of the digital self'. *The International Journal of Media and Culture*, 15(2), 110–25. https://doi.org/10.4324/9780429429187

Bowman, E. (2021). '"Charlie Bit Me" will remain on YouTube after NFT auction switcheroo'. *NPR*, 30 May. https://www.npr.org/2021/05/30/1001627869/charlie-bit-me-will-remain-on-youtube-after-nft-auction-switcheroo

Bramwell, K. and K. Allen (2019). 'Social outcry over video of mum kicking daughter'. *BBC News*, 10 April. https://www.bbc.com/news/blogs-trending-47879848

Burroughs, B. (2017). 'YouTube kids: The app economy and mobile parenting'. *Social Media + Society*, 3(2), 1–8. https://doi.org/10.1177/2056305117707189

Burroughs, B. and G. Feller (2021). 'The emergence and ethics of child-created content as media industries'. In L. Green, D. Holloway, K. Stevenson, T. Leaver and L. Haddon (eds.), *The Routledge Companion to Digital Media and Children*. Abingdon: Routledge, 217–25. https://doi.org/10.4324/9781351004107

Cabbuag, S.L. and C. Abidin (2024). 'TikTok "dogshows" and the amplification of online incivility among Gen Z influencers in the Philippines'. *International Journal of Cultural Studies* (online first). https://journals.sagepub.com/doi/10.1177/13678779241302826

CGTN (2018). 'Internet fame brings Gavin the meme boy to China'. *CGTN*, 20 August. https://news.cgtn.com/news/3d3d514d34456a4e79457a6333566d54/share_p.html

Chalklen, C. and H. Anderson (2017). 'Mothering on Facebook: Exploring the privacy/openness paradox'. *Social Media + Society*, 3(2), 1–13. https://doi.org/10.1177/2056305117707187

Chen, L. (2018). 'The American "fake smile boy" China genuinely loves'. *South China Morning Post*, 8 November. https://www.scmp.com/news/china/society/article/2172220/american-fake-smile-boy-china-genuinely-loves

Coast, D. and J. Fox (2015). 'Rumour and politics'. *History Compass*, 13(5), 222–34. https://doi.org/10.1111/hic3.12234

Cord-Cruz, N., C. Bend and O. Scott (2024). 'Viral sensations: Where are the Baby Shark kids now?' *The Sun*, 17 September. https://www.the-sun.com/entertainment/celebrity/8725381/where-baby-shark-kids-now-video/

Corn Kid (2022). 'Cameo'. https://www.cameo.com/cornkid

Cotter, K. (2018). 'Playing the visibility game: How digital influencers and algorithms negotiate influence on Instagram'. *New Media & Society*, 21(4), 895–913. https://doi.org/10.1177/1461444818815684

Craig, D. and S. Cunningham (2017). 'Toy unboxing: Living in a(n unregulated) material world'. *Media International Australia*, 163(1), 77–86. https://doi.org/10.1177/1329878X17693700

Cunningham, S. and D. Craig (2019). *Social Media Entertainment: The New Intersection of Hollywood and Silicon Valley*. New York: NYU Press. https://nyupress.org/9781479846894/social-media-entertainment/

Das, R. (2019). *Early Motherhood in Digital Societies: Ideals, Anxieties and Ties of the Perinatal*. Abingdon: Taylor & Francis. https://doi.org/10.4324/9781315167725

De Leyn, T., R. De Wolf, M. Vanden Abeele and L. De Marez (2022). 'In-between child's play and teenage pop culture: tweens, TikTok & privacy'. *Journal of Youth Studies*, 25(8), 1108–25. https://doi.org/10.1080/13676261.2021.1939286

Deem, A. (2023). '"Feminine, not feminist": Trad truth-making on social media'. *Ethnologia Europaea*, 53(2), 1–20. https://doi.org/10.16995/ee.8841

Dickson, E.J. (2022). 'A toddler on TikTok is spawning a massive mom-led movement'. *Rolling Stone*, 20 July. https://www.rollingstone.com/culture/culture-news/tiktok-wren-eleanor-moms-controversy-1385182/

Digital Child (2024). 'About'. *Digital Child.* https://digitalchild.org.au/about/

Eh Bee (2014). 'Let's get crazy for new years! #NYEonVine'. Vine, 31 December. *Deleted.* https://vine.co/v/OwTOez0W6wg

Eh Bee (2015). 'Let's get crazy for new years!' Vine, 31 December. *Deleted.* https://vine.co/v/iqVveY1QpzI

Ellen (2017). '#SophiaGraceAndRosie'. *ellentv.com.* [Link since removed]

Evans, A. (2021). 'Charlie Bit Me NFT sale: Brothers to pay for university with auction money'. *BBC News*, 3 June. https://www.bbc.com/news/newsbeat-57333990

Farley, S. (2019). 'On the nature of gossip, reputation, and power inequality'. In F. Giardini and R. Wittek (eds.), *The Oxford Handbook of Gossip and Reputation* (online edn). Oxford Academic. https://doi.org/10.1093/oxfordhb/9780190494087.013.18

Feldman, B. (2016). 'Who is Gavin? And why has he taken over Twitter?' *New York Magazine*, 12 August. https://nymag.com/intelligencer/2016/08/meet-gavin-the-five-year-old-meme-star.html

Feller, G. and B. Burroughs (2021). 'Branding kidfluencers: Regulating content and advertising on YouTube'. *Television & New Media*, 23(6), 575–92. https://doi.org/10.1177/15274764211052882

Friedman, M. and S.L. Calixte (eds.) (2009). *Mothering and Blogging: The Radical Act of the Mommyblog.* Ontario: Demeter Press.

https://demeterpress.org/books/mothering-and-blogging-the-radical-act-of-the-mommyblog/

Fuchs, C. (2015). Social media surveillance. In S. Coleman and D. Freelon (eds.), *Handbook of Digital Politics*. Cheltenham: Edward Elgar, 395–414. https://doi.org/10.4337/9781782548768.00034

Goffman, E. (1956). *The Presentation of Self in Everyday Life*. London: Penguin Books. https://www.penguin.com.au/books/the-presentation-of-self-in-everyday-life-9780385094023

Green, L., D. Holloway, K. Stevenson, T. Leaver and L. Haddon (eds.) (2021). *The Routledge Companion to Digital Media and Children*. Abingdon: Routledge. https://www.routledge.com/The-Routledge-Companion-to-Digital-Media-and-Children/Green-Holloway-Stevenson-Leaver-Haddon/p/book/9780367559069?srsltid=AfmBOoql_zIIdgBtFJxhrSc8doxxsDd1s8YUw4odvkL4vFNJ6y2ONms1

Griffith, M. and Z. Papacharissi (2010). 'Looking for you: An analysis of video blogs'. *First Monday*, 15(1). https://doi.org/10.5210/fm.v15i1.2769

Grindstaff, L. (2002). *The Money Shot: Trash, Class, and the Making of TV Talk Shows*. Chicago: University of Chicago Press. https://press.uchicago.edu/ucp/books/book/chicago/M/bo3630693.html

Gunter, B. (2021). *Children and Television Consumption in the Digital Era: Use, Impact and Regulation*. Abingdon: Routledge. https://www.routledge.com/Children-and-Television-Consumption-in-the-Digital-Era-Use-Impact-and-Regulation/Gunter/p/book/9780367473495?srsltid=AfmBOoq8X8VLfJl2d0OJMb_LbtmjhiFNlBKKUC5tEaQQwNm4K9x1CA6X

Haley, K. (2020). 'Sharenting and the (potential) right to be forgotten'. *Indiana Law Journal*, 95, 1005. https://heinonline.org/HOL/P?h=hein.journals/indana95&i=1029

Heller, C. (2023). 'Ellen star Sophia Grace gives birth to her first baby'. *E! Online*, 6 March. https://www.eonline.com/news/1366904/ellen-star-sophia-grace-gives-birth-to-her-first-baby

Hern, A. (2018). 'FamilyOFive: YouTube bans "pranksters" after child abuse conviction'. *The Guardian*, 20 July. https://www.theguardian.com/technology/2018/jul/19/youtube-bans-familyofive-pranksters-michael-heather-martin-child-abuse-conviction

Huang, E. (2019). 'China is cracking down on child modeling after a video showed a mom kicking her toddler'. *Quartz*, 10 May. https://qz.com/1616181/china-is-cracking-down-on-child-modeling

Hudders, L. and E. Beuckels (2024). 'Children making big money: The implications of Kidfluencing as new form of child labor'. *Journal of Children and Media*, 18(4), 638–45. https://doi.org/10.1080/17482798.2024.2404729

Hudders, L., S. De Jans and E. Beuckels (2024). 'Kidfluencers and the commodification of childhood: A comprehensive review and research agenda in contemporary entertainment'. In B. Feijoo and E. Fernández Gómez (eds.), *Advertising Literacy for Young Audiences in the Digital Age: A Critical Attitude to Embedded Formats*. Cham: Springer, 65–83. https://doi.org/10.1007/978-3-031-55736-1_5

Hunter, A. (2016). 'Monetizing the mommy: Mommy blogs and the audience commodity'. *Information, Communication & Society*, 19(9), 1306–20. https://doi.org/10.1080/1369118X.2016.1187642

Hutchinson, J. (2019). 'Digital first personality: Automation and influence within evolving media ecologies'. *Convergence: The International Journal of Research into New Media Technologies*, 26(5–6), 1284–300. https://doi.org/10.1177/1354856519858921

Ingber, A.S. and C.C. Su (2024). 'Protecting children of the TikTok era: A discourse analysis in the absence of law'. *Policy & Internet* (online first). https://doi.org/10.1002/poi3.431

Johnson, D. (2019). *Transgenerational Media Industries: Adults, Children, and the Reproduction of Culture*. Ann Arbor: University of Michigan Press. https://doi.org/10.3998/mpub.9894091

JTBC Entertainment (2016). 'Halfmoon Friends'. YouTube. https://www.youtube.com/@JTBCentertainment/search?query=halfmoon%20friends

Kaur, H. (2022). '"Tradwives" promote a lifestyle that evokes the 1950s. But their nostalgia is not without controversy'. *CNN*, 27 December. https://edition.cnn.com/2022/12/27/us/tradwife-1950s-nostalgia-tiktok-cec/index.html

Kemp, S. (2011). 'Digital 2011: Singapore'. *DataReportal*, 23 December. https://datareportal.com/reports/digital-2011-singapore

Kennedy, Ü. (2024). '"THESE VLOGS AREN'T REAL": Managing authenticity and privacy as family influencers'. *M/C Journal*, 27(6). https://doi.org/10.5204/mcj.3080

Kilkenny, K. (2024). 'Gavin Newsom signs bills protecting compensation for child influencers'. *The Hollywood Reporter*, 26 September. https://www.hollywoodreporter.com/business/business-news/child-influencer-protection-bills-signed-law-california-1236013469/

Kindelan, K. (2022). 'Parents remove videos of their kids from TikTok after "Wren Eleanor" warning'. *ABC News*, 28 July. https://abcnews.go.com/GMA/Family/wren-eleanor-tiktok-trend-sees-parents-removing-photos/story?id=87486106

Kumar, P. (2020). 'Child influencing is work, but it's not automatically dangerous: A new French law fails to understand that'. *Slate*, 28 October. https://slate.com/technology/2020/10/french-law-child-influencers-labor-protections.html

Lagerwey, J. (2016). *Postfeminist Celebrity and Motherhood: Brand Mom*. New York: Routledge. https://doi.org/10.4324/9781315636665

Lange, P. (2014). *Kids on YouTube: Technical Identities and Digital Literacies*. Abingdon: Routledge. https://doi.org/10.4324/9781315425733

Larsen, M., C. Abidin, C. Epps-Robertson, M. Cho and C. Anderson (2020). 'Kpop: Fandom, politics, digital influence'. *Fan Studies Network North America 2020 Conference*, online, 13–17 October.

Lawson, C.E. (2020). 'Skin deep: Callout strategies, influencers, and racism in the online beauty community'. *New Media & Society* (online first). https://doi.org/10.1177/1461444820904697

Lawson, V. (2024). *Snarking to Repair: A Mixed-Methods Analysis of r/FundieSnarkUncensored* (Doctoral dissertation, Michigan State University). https://d.lib.msu.edu/etd/51711

Leaver, T. and C. Abidin (2017). 'When exploiting kids for cash goes wrong on YouTube: The lessons of DaddyOFive'. *The Conversation*, 2 May. https://theconversation.com/when-exploiting-kids-for-cash-goes-wrong-on-youtube-the-lessons-of-daddyofive-76932

Lee, J. and C. Abidin (2021). 'Backdoor advertising scandals, Yingyeo culture, and cancel culture among YouTube Influencers in South Korea'. *New Media & Society*, 26(1), 405–25. https://doi.org/10.1177/14614448211061829

Lee, J. and C. Abidin (2022). 'Oegugin influencers and pop nationalism through government campaigns: Regulating foreign-nationals in the South Korean YouTube ecology'. *Policy & Internet*, 14(3), 541–57. https://doi.org/10.1002/poi3.319

Lee, J. and C. Abidin (2023). 'Ella Gross and child social media stars: Rising to fame through K-pop idol trainee systems, mixed raceness, and tabloid cycle controversies'. In K. Khiun Liew, S. J. Lee and K. Korroch (eds.), *Women We Love in and around K-Pop and K-Drama in the Hallyu Era*. Hong Kong: Hong Kong University Press, 71–94. https://www.degruyter.com/document/doi/10.1515/9789888842650-009/html

Lee, J., T. Leaver and C. Abidin (2024). 'Child idols in South Korea and beyond: Manufacturing young stars at the intersection of the K-pop and influencer industries'. *New Media & Society* (online first). https://doi.org/10.1177/14614448241295718

Lehto, M. (2020). 'Bad is the new good: Negotiating bad motherhood in Finnish mommy blogs'. *Feminist Media Studies*, 20(5), 657–71. https://doi.org/10.1080/14680777.2019.1642224

Leidig, E. (2023). *The Women of the Far Right: Social Media Influencers and Online Radicalization*. New York: Columbia University Press. https://doi.org/10.7312/leid21016

Lemish, D. (ed.) (2022). *The Routledge International Handbook of Children, Adolescents and Media*. New York: Routledge. https://doi.org/10.4324/9781003118824

Li, L. (2019). 'Abuse of child model raises questions about labor law'. *China Daily*, 12 April. https://www.chinadaily.com.cn/a/201904/12/WS5caffa17a3104842260b5d5f.html

Library of Congress (2020). 'France: Parliament adopts law to protect child "influencers" on social media'. *Library of Congress*, 30 October. https://www.loc.gov/item/global-legal-monitor/2020-10-30/france-parliament-adopts-law-to-protect-child-influencers-on-social-media/

Lim, A. (2024). 'The kid from the "Baby Shark" music video is now 15, and he looks just like a K-pop idol'. *Today Online*, 13 July. https://www.todayonline.com/8days/kid-baby-shark-music-video-now-15-and-he-looks-just-k-pop-idol-2457876

Littler, J. (2013). 'The rise of the "yummy mummy": Popular conservatism and the neoliberal maternal in contemporary British culture'. *Communication, Culture and Critique*, 6(2), 227–43. https://doi.org/10.1111/cccr.12010

Livingstone, S. (2018). 'Audiences in an age of datafication: Critical questions for media research'. *Television & New Media*, 20(2), 170–83. https://doi.org/10.1177/1527476418811118

Locker, M. (2020). 'Families travel back in time with childhood photos for the "I'm just a kid" challenge'. *Time*, 15 April. https://time.com/5821238/im-just-a-kid-challenge-explained/

Lopez, L.K. (2009). 'The radical act of "mommy blogging": Redefining motherhood through the blogosphere'. *New Media & Society*, 11(5), 729–47. https://doi.org/10.1177/1461444809105349

Love, N.S. (2020). 'Shield maidens, fashy femmes, and tradwives: Feminism, patriarchy, and right-wing populism'. *Frontiers in Sociology*. https://doi.org/10.3389/fsoc.2020.619572

MacCannell, D. (1973). 'Staged authenticity: Arrangements of social space in tourist settings'. *American Journal of Sociology*, 79(3), 589–603. https://www.jstor.org/stable/2776259

Malatzky, C.A.R. (2017). 'Australian women's complex engagement with the yummy mummy discourse and the bodily ideals of good motherhood'. *Women's Studies International Forum*, 62, 25–33. https://doi.org/10.1016/j.wsif.2017.04.001

Markham, A. (2012). 'Fabrication as ethical practice: Qualitative inquiry in ambiguous internet contexts'. *Information, Communication & Society*, 15(3), 334–53. https://doi.org/10.1080/1369118X.2011.641993

Maris, E., R. Caplan and H. Thach (2024). 'Taking back and giving back on TikTok: Algorithmic mutual aid in the platform economy'. *New Media & Society*, 4071–89. https://doi.org/10.1177/14614448241238396

Marsh, J. (2004). 'The techno-literacy practices of young children'. *Journal of Early Childhood Research*, 2(1), 51–66. https://doi.org/10.1177/1476718X0421003

Marsh, J. (2016). '"Unboxing" videos: Co-construction of the child as cyberflâneur'. *Discourse: Studies in the Cultural Politics of Education*, 37(3), 369–80. https://doi.org/10.1080/01596306.2015.1041457

Martínez, C. and T. Olsson (2019). 'Making sense of YouTubers: How Swedish children construct and negotiate the YouTuber Misslisibell as a girl celebrity'. *Journal of Children and Media*, 13(1), 36–52. https://doi.org/10.1080/17482798.2018.1517656

Marwick, A.E. (2013). *Status Update: Celebrity, Publicity, and Branding in the Social Media Age*. New Haven, CT: Yale University Press. https://yalebooks.yale.edu/book/9780300209389/status-update/

Masia, L. (2024). 'The parents of TikTok's fully conscious baby confirmed how old their strangely cognisant bub is'. *Pedestrian TV*, 24 May. https://www.pedestrian.tv/entertainment/tiktok-fully-conscious-baby-explained/

Mattheis, A.A. (2021). '#TradCulture: Reproducing whiteness and neo-fascism through gendered discourse online'. In S. Hunter and C. van der Westhuizen (eds.), *Routledge Handbook of Critical Studies in Whiteness*. Abingdon: Routledge, 91–101. https://doi.org/10.4324/9780429355769

McCusker, K. (2025). 'The sad beige aesthetic: Why has the world suddenly turned taupe?' *The Guardian*, 9 January.

https://www.theguardian.com/lifeandstyle/2025/jan/09/the-sad-beige-aesthetic-why-has-the-world-suddenly-turned-taupe

McLaughlin, K. (2024). 'Unpacking the beige kids decor controversy rocking the internet'. *Architectural Digest*, 17 October. https://www.architecturaldigest.com/story/the-beige-kids-decor-controversy-rocking-the-design-world

Milner, R.M. (2018). *The World Made Meme: Public Conversations and Participatory Media*. Cambridge, MA: The MIT Press. https://mitpress.mit.edu/9780262535229/the-world-made-meme/

Mina, A.X. (2019). *Memes to Movements: How the World's Most Viral Media is Changing Social Protest and Power*. Boston: Beacon Press. https://www.penguinrandomhouse.com/books/567159/memes-to-movements-by-an-xiao-mina/

NBC (n.d.). 'Little big shots'. *NBC.com*. https://www.nbc.com/little-big-shots

Ni, D. (2019). 'Mother apologizes for kicking 3-year-old child model'. *Sixth Tone*, 11 April. https://www.sixthtone.com/news/1003828

Nicioli, T. (2024). 'Here's what child development experts think about the "beige mom" trend'. *CNN*, 5 December. https://edition.cnn.com/2024/12/05/health/sad-beige-mom-aesthetic-wellness/index.html

Nicoll, B. and B. Nansen (2018). 'Mimetic production in YouTube toy unboxing videos'. *Social Media + Society*, 4(3), 1–12. https://doi.org/10.1177/2056305118790761

Nover, S. (2021). 'Charlie Bit Me won't be leaving YouTube after all'. *Quartz*, 27 May. https://qz.com/2014092/charlie-bit-me-wont-be-leaving-youtube-after-all-father-says

O'Donohoe, S. (2006). 'Yummy mummies: The clamor of glamour in advertising to mothers'. *Advertising & Society Review*, 7(3). https://doi.org/10.1353/asr.2007.0006

Oldenburg, R. (1999). *The Great Good Place: Cafes, Coffee Shops, Bookstores, Bars, Hair Salons, and Other Hangouts at the Heart of a Community*. London: Hachette Books.

Organ, C. (2022). 'Why the Wren Eleanor controversy makes parents so uncomfortable'. *Motherly,* 25 August. https://www.mother.ly/life/motherly-stories/wren-eleanor-social-media/

Orton-Johnson, K. (2017). 'Mummy blogs and representations of motherhood: "Bad mummies" and their readers'. *Social Media + Society,* 3(2), 1–10. https://doi.org/10.1177/2056305117707186

Ozduzen, O., N. Ferenczi and I. Holmes (2023). '"Let us teach our children": Online racism and everyday far-right ideologies on TikTok'. *Visual Studies,* 38(5), 834–50. https://doi.org/10.1080/1472586X.2023.2274890

Phillips, W. (2016). *This is Why We Can't Have Nice Things: Mapping the Relationship between Online Trolling and Mainstream Culture.* Cambridge, MA: The MIT Press. https://mitpress.mit.edu/9780262529877/this-is-why-we-cant-have-nice-things/

Prema, S. (2020). '"I couldn't stand them!" Matthew "Matty J" Johnson recreates childhood photos for the "I'm Just A Kid" TikTok challenge – but fans keep commenting about his ears which appear noticeably different'. *Daily Mail,* 20 April. https://www.dailymail.co.uk/tvshowbiz/article-8236281/Matthew-Matty-J-Johnson-does-Im-Just-Kid-challenge-fans-commenting-ears.html

Prinds, C., H. Nikolajsen and B. Folmann (2020). 'Yummy mummy – The ideal of not looking like a mother'. *Women and Birth,* 33(3), e266–e273. https://doi.org/10.1016/j.wombi.2019.05.009

Radics, G. and C. Abidin (2022). 'Racial harmony and sexual violence: Uneven regulation and legal protection gaps for influencers in Singapore'. *Policy & Internet,* 14(3), 597–617. https://doi.org/10.1002/poi3.320

Rauchberg, J. and J. Maddox (2024). '"She's my bitch eating crackers": Influencer snark and the digital gossip economy'. *Feminist Media Studies* (online first). https://doi.org/10.1080/14680777.2024.2430462

Reeves, J. (2012). 'If you see something, say something: Lateral surveillance and the uses of responsibility'. *Surveillance & Society,* 10(3/4). https://doi.org/10.24908/ss.v10i3/4.4209

Rieffel, Y. (2023). 'French MPs examine bill on children's right to privacy on social media'. *Le Monde,* 5 March. https://www.lemonde.fr/en/france/article/2023/03/05/french-mp-proposes-bill-to-protect-children-s-privacy-on-social-media_6018268_7.html

Rodie, C. (2017). 'What the "yummy mummy" label forgets about women's lives'. *Sydney Morning Herald,* 22 June. https://www.smh.com.au/lifestyle/life-and-relationships/what-the-yummy-mummy-label-forgets-about-womens-lives-20170621-gwvigr.html

Rodriguez, A. and X. Zhao (2024). 'Pushing against the panic: Considering the positives of TikTok and children'. *International Journal of Cultural Studies* (online first). https://doi.org/10.1177/13678779241276011

Rojek, C. (2001). *Celebrity.* London: Reaktion Books. https://reaktionbooks.co.uk/work/celebrity

Rotimi, I.R., S-F. Yap and B. Wooliscroft (2024). 'Unboxing the child influencer paradoxes: A research agenda'. *Journal of Marketing Management,* 40(11–12), 1030–57. https://doi.org/10.1080/0267257X.2024.2405597

Sarwatay, D., J. Lee and D.B. Valdovinos (2023). 'Exploring children's TikTok cultures in India: Negotiating access, uses, and experiences under restrictive parental mediation'. *Media International Australia,* 186(1), 48–65. https://doi.org/10.1177/1329878X221127037

Scanlan, R. (2024). 'Bizarre reason the "Four Seasons Orlando" baby has gone viral'. *News.com.au,* 22 May. https://www.news.com.au/lifestyle/parenting/babies/bizarre-reason-the-four-seasons-orlando-baby-has-gone-viral/news-story/0c220152cdc3b5b22613cd1b2090a7f4

Schwartz, O. (2019). 'Meet Gavin, the eight-year-old with a face shared more than 1bn times'. *The Guardian,* 28 January. https://www.theguardian.com/lifeandstyle/2019/jan/28/gavin-thomas-meme-internet-son-social-media

Senft, T.M. (2008). *Camgirls: Celebrity and Community in the Age of Social Networks.* New York: Peter Lang.

Shaw, F. (2012). 'The politics of blogs: Theories of discursive activism online'. *Media International Australia*, 142(1), 41–9. https://doi.org/10.1177/1329878X1214200106

Shaw, F. (2013). 'Emotional investments: Australian feminist blogging and affective networks'. In T. Benski and E. Fisher (eds.), *Internet and Emotions*. New York: Routledge, 211–24. https://doi.org/10.4324/9780203427408

Shifman, L. (2013). *Memes in Digital Culture*. Cambridge, MA: The MIT Press. https://doi.org/10.7551/mitpress/9429.001.0001

Siibak, A. and K. Traks (2019). 'The dark sides of sharenting'. *Catalan Journal of Communication & Cultural Studies*, 11(1), 115–21. https://doi.org/10.1386/cjcs.11.1.115_1

Smith, J.K. and E.A. Mendelson (2024). 'Parasocial parenting, adoption, and monetization of the "internet parent" with the Griswolds on TikTok'. *International Journal of Cultural Studies* (online first). https://doi.org/10.1177/13678779241288619

Smith-Engelhardt, J. (2020). 'See Simple Plan celebrate a milestone by doing their own TikTok challenge'. *Alternative Press*, 28 May. https://www.altpress.com/simple-plan-im-just-a-kid-certified-platinum-tiktok-challenge/

SophiaGraceTheArtist (n.d.). 'About'. Facebook. *Deleted*. https://www.facebook.com/pg/SophiaGraceTheArtist/about/?ref=page_internal

Soriano-Ayala, E., M. Bonillo Díaz and V.C. Cala (2023). 'TikTok and child hypersexualization: Analysis of videos and narratives of minors'. *The Journal of Social Media in Society*, 18(2), 210–30. https://doi.org/10.1080/15546128.2022.2096734

Sweat, Z. (2022). 'Vine star and meme icon Gavin Thomas reflects on his viral internet fame eight years later'. *Know Your Meme*. https://knowyourmeme.com/editorials/interviews/vine-star-and-meme-icon-gavin-thomas-reflects-on-his-viral-internet-fame-eight-years-later

Sykes, I. (2024). 'From "girlboss" to #stayathomegirlfriend: The romanticisation of domestic labour on TikTok'. *European Journal of Cultural Studies* (online first). https://journals.sagepub.com/doi/full/10.1177/13675494241285643

Sykes, S. and V. Hopner (2024). 'Tradwives: Right-wing social media influencers'.

Journal of Contemporary Ethnography, 53(4), 453–87. https://doi.org/10.1177/08912416241246273

Taylor, Z.A. and C. Abidin (2024). 'Where are all the Black girls on TikTok? Exploring in-group community and (in)visibility through #BlackGirlTikTok'. *International Journal of Cultural Studies* (online first). https://journals.sagepub.com/doi/epdf/10.1177/13678779241276751

The Economist. (2024). '#Tradwives, the real housewives of the internet, have gone viral'. *The Economist*, 15 May. https://www.economist.com/culture/2024/05/15/tradwives-the-real-housewives-of-the-internet-have-gone-viral

Titan Digital Media. (2024). 'Our work'. *Titan Digital Media.* https://titandigitalmedia.com/#OUR_WORK

Trezise, B. (2023). *Performing Contemporary Childhoods: Being and Becoming a Viral Child.* London: Taylor & Francis. https://doi.org/10.4324/9781003289685

Trottier, D. and D. Lyon (2012). 'Key features of social media surveillance'. In C. Fuchs, K. Boersma, A. Albrechtslund and M. Sandoval (eds.), *Internet and Surveillance.* New York: Routledge, 215–33. https://doi.org/10.4324/9780203806432

Turner, G. (2010). *Ordinary People and the Media: The Demotic Turn.* Los Angeles: Sage. https://doi.org/10.4135/9781446269565

Turvy, A. (2024). 'Reading latent values and priorities in TikTok's community guidelines for children'. *International Journal of Cultural Studies* (online first). https://doi.org/10.1177/13678779241276884

Turvy, A. and C. Abidin (2025). 'Patchwork governance on KidTok: Balancing regulation and community norms'. *Policy and Internet,* 17(2), 1–14. https://doi.org/10.1002/poi3.70003

UK Parliament (2021). 'European Scrutiny Committee: Twelfth Report of Session 2021–22: Documents considered by the Committee on

17 November 2021'. House of Commons, 17 November. https://committees.parliament.uk/publications/7931/documents/82135/default/

UK Parliament (2022). 'Influencer culture: Lights, camera, inaction? Government response to the Committee's twelfth report of session 2021–22'. Digital, Culture, Media and Sport Committee. https://committees.parliament.uk/publications/28742/documents/173531/default/

Verdoodt, V., S. van der Hof and M. Leiser (2020). 'Child labour and online protection in a world of influencers'. In C. Goanta and S. Ranchordás (eds.), *The Regulation of Social Media Influencers*. Cheltenham: Edward Elgar, 98–124. https://doi.org/10.4337/9781788978286.00013

Vizcaíno-Verdú, A. and C. Abidin (2023). 'TeachTok: Teachers of TikTok, micro-celebrification, and fun learning communities'. *Teaching and Teacher Education*, 123, 103978. https://doi.org/10.1016/j.tate.2022.103978

Vizcaíno-Verdú, A., P. De-Casas-Moreno and D. Jaramillo-Dent (2022). 'Thanks for joining our life: Intimacy as performativity on YouTube parenting vlogs'. *Information Professional*, 31(4). https://doi.org/10.3145/epi.2022.jul.07

Yahoo News Australia & Agencies (2019). 'Brutal video emerges of mum kicking social media child star'. *Yahoo! News*, 11 April. https://au.news.yahoo.com/brutal-video-emerges-mum-kicking-social-media-child-star-074304118.html

Yip, J.A., M.E. Schweitzer and S. Nurmohamed (2018). 'Trash-talking: Competitive incivility motivates rivalry, performance, and unethical behavior'. *Organizational Behavior and Human Decision Processes*, 144, 125–44. https://doi.org/10.1016/j.obhdp.2017.06.002

Zamolo, Z. (2017). 'How to get on The Ellen Show w/ Sophia Grace!!'. YouTube, 27 July. *Deleted*. https://www.youtube.com/watch?v=-vK21qPujmI&feature=youtu.be

Zeng, J. and C. Abidin (2021). '"#OkBoomer, time to meet the Zoomers": Studying the memeification of intergenerational politics on TikTok'. *Information, Communication & Society*, 24(16), 2459–81. https://doi.org/10.1080/1369118X.2021.1961007

@clicknetwork (2017). 'New popin' cookin' – Xiaxue's guide to life: EP202'. YouTube, 14 July. https://www.youtube.com/watch?v=sFQxOV54xNk&feature=youtu.be

@deksorkrao (2016). 'BLACKPINK – "불장난 (Playing with Fire)" M/V | Parody cover by DEKSORKRAO from Thailand'. YouTube, 9 December. https://www.youtube.com/watch?v=NxWrPah_m3U

@deksorkrao (2018). 'BLACKPINK x DEKSORKRAO – "마지막처럼 As if it's your last" M_V'. YouTube, 14 January. https://www.youtube.com/watch?v=_sME8KY8beU

@deksorkrao (2022). 'BLACKPINK – "Pink Venom" M/V cover | by DEKSORKRAO from Thailand'. YouTube, 29 August. https://www.youtube.com/watch?v=nE0ITxDkH3g&list=PL637FmkuxKpFnggPtJQNFeTmPln5pcBHi

@deksorkrao (2024). '@deksorkrao'. YouTube. https://www.youtube.com/@deksorkrao

@ehbeefamily (2014). 'KidzBop Vine compilation—Eh Bee Family'. YouTube, 16 September. *Deleted.* https://www.youtube.com/watch?v=S5OwVT-1tQw

@ehbeefamily (2016a). 'Basically what Mama Bee looks like'. Twitter, 28 June. *Deleted.* https://twitter.com/EhBeeFamily/status/747577717625757696

@ehbeefamily (2016b). 'I lied to my wife – Family Q&A'. YouTube, 28 January. https://www.youtube.com/watch?v=g8cWgwxRnZA

@ehbeefamily (2024a). 'Eh Bee Family'. Instagram. https://www.instagram.com/ehbeefamily/

@ehbeefamily (2024b). 'Eh Bee Family'. YouTube. https://www.youtube.com/@ehbeefamily/videos

@ellendegeneres (2023). 'Tea Time is cuter with Tutus. Watch every episode of Tea Time with @therealsophiagrace & @rosiergm on my YouTube channel'. Instagram, 29 June. https://www.instagram.com/reel/CuFfRlONh-G/

@fallontonight (2012). 'Hashtags: #OopsMyBad (Late Night with Jimmy Fallon)'. YouTube, 27 September. https://www.youtube.com/watch?v=NEvjS2JhpdA

@iNabber (2024). 'Wren Eleanor: The TikTok mom who is exploiting her child for predators'. YouTube, 28 March. https://www.youtube.com/watch?v=PA4DHz7Cs_M

@jebbey (2024a). 'Jebbey Family'. YouTube. https://www.youtube.com/@jebbey/videos

@jebbey (2024b). 'Taking my 5-year-old daughter on a day out without my husband'. YouTube, 19 November. https://www.youtube.com/watch?v=N7ERrQrxIFY

@jebbey (2024c). 'Our daughter answers questions everyone has been asking'. YouTube, 14 October. https://www.youtube.com/watch?v=bSziHtt1jRo

@jebbey (2024d). 'Surprising our 5-year-old daughter with a Pokémon themed party!'. YouTube, 19 September. https://www.youtube.com/watch?v=tdUGYPLk2gs

@jebbey (2024e). 'Surprising my daughter with a mermaid themed room in Hong Kong'. YouTube, 30 August. https://www.youtube.com/watch?v=7VxshE5OCc0

@JessiiVee (2017). 'Ghost hunting at a haunted zoo! | Collab with Sophia Grace'. YouTube, 17 August. https://www.youtube.com/watch?v=HquoXwKrJ_g&feature=youtu.be

@jianhao (2020). 'A day in JianHao's life as a dad (in quarantine)'. YouTube, 17 May. https://www.youtube.com/watch?v=FhkqKiNINZg

@jianhao (2024). 'Jianhao'. YouTube. https://www.youtube.com/@jianhao/videos

@jianhao2 (2023). 'Preparing my 4-year-old daughter's dream birthday'. YouTube, 26 September. https://www.youtube.com/watch?v=ALlvEMG3muQ

@jianhao2 (2024). 'Jianhao2'. YouTube. https://www.youtube.com/@jianhao2/videos

@JimmyKimmelLive (2011). 'YouTube challenge – I told my kids I ate all their Halloween candy'. YouTube, 3 November.

https://www.youtube.com/watch?v=_YQpbzQ6gzs&list=PLs4hTtftqnlBuue-6Q1WKBHVAjLKV3H_D

@kbsworldtv (2017a). 'Seungjae pours water into his dad to cure his hangover! [The Return of Superman / 2017.07.09]'. YouTube, 9 July. https://www.youtube.com/watch?v=5YULFeCPKdw

@kbsworldtv (2017b). 'Seungjae's tears for the beggar hyungs "I'm going to feed them" [The Return of Superman/2017.06.04]'. YouTube, 4 June. https://www.youtube.com/watch?v=I9JsUiK-Jos

@kbsworldtv (2017c). 'Cute Seungjae cries out for help! "Please don't eat my crab!" [The Return of Superman/2017.07.23]'. YouTube, 23 July. https://www.youtube.com/watch?v=2vCyxztOY5U

@kbsworldtv (2017d). 'Seungjae's linguistic skills that surprised everyone [The Return of Superman / 2017.02.26]'. YouTube, 27 February. https://www.youtube.com/watch?v=mFCzMWRR_3U

@kbsworldtv (2017e). 'Selling empty bottles to buy ice-cream!!! [The Return of Superman / 2017.04.09]'. YouTube, 8 April. https://www.youtube.com/watch?v=4ZT24zNQChk

@kbsworldtv (2018a). 'Seungjae finally reunites with Uncle Liu Yihao in Taiwan!! [The Return of Superman/2018.07.08]'. YouTube, 8 July. https://www.youtube.com/watch?v=-VA0b98qpEI

@kbsworldtv (2018b). 'Seungjae "Please take good care of Dokdo Island ♥" [The Return of Superman/2018.06.24]'. YouTube, 26 June. https://www.youtube.com/watch?v=oPGYZ_cYSi0

@LADIESFIRSTTVSG (2019). 'Baby's nursery room tour!' YouTube, 15 November. https://www.youtube.com/watch?v=sJxxw-Wcd5U

@LADIESFIRSTTVSG (2024). 'LADIESFIRSTTVSG'. YouTube. https://www.youtube.com/@LADIESFIRSTTVSG/videos

@realitychangers (2010). 'Home | Edward Sharpe and The Magnetic Zeros acoustic cover | Narvaez music covers | Reality Changers'. YouTube, 31 December. https://www.youtube.com/watch?v=L64c5vT3NBw

@realitychangers (2011a). 'Eliana and the dead fish!! – Vlog 061 | Reality Changers'. YouTube, 17 August. https://www.youtube.com/watch?v=mQ3Lyy4Ywng

@realitychangers (2011b). 'Eli likes netflix and birds! – Vlog 096 | Reality Changers'. YouTube, 12 November. https://www.youtube.com/watch?v=lE_qC-G9p7I

@realitychangers (2014a). 'Come watch us perform! | The Family Vlog | Reality Changers'. YouTube, 30 August. https://www.youtube.com/watch?v=nsQ0S9Qf7IM

@realitychangers (2014b). 'What happened at Vidcon? | The Family Vlog | Reality Changers'. YouTube, 5 July. https://www.youtube.com/watch?v=2U5HrUo2xl8

@RyansWorld (2024). 'Ryan's World'. YouTube. https://www.youtube.com/@RyansWorld/videos

@SophiaGrace (2011a). 'Nicki Minaj – Super Bass by Sophia Grace Brownlee | Sophia Grace'. YouTube, 19 September. https://www.youtube.com/watch?v=C7hTAp6KrGY

@SophiaGrace (2011b). 'About'. YouTube, 15 September. https://www.youtube.com/user/SophiaGraceBrownlee/about

@SophiaGrace (2011c). 'Sophia Grace & Rosie sing with One Direction | Sophia Grace'. YouTube, 12 December. https://www.youtube.com/watch?v=aEWkmO9qXxM

@SophiaGrace (2013). 'Sophia Grace "Girls Just Gotta Have Fun" official music video | Sophia Grace'. YouTube, 31 May. https://www.youtube.com/watch?v=SMpL6JKF5Ww

@SophiaGrace (2015). 'Sophia Grace – "Best Friends" official music video | Sophia Grace'. YouTube, 7 January. https://www.youtube.com/watch?v=DdsIVUuO7GM

@SophiaGrace (2016a). 'Sophia Grace | Meets "Bratayley" at Music al.ly'. YouTube, 2 December. https://www.youtube.com/watch?v=P727sKL6d3I

@SophiaGrace (2016b). 'Sophia Grace – My bedroom chat | Sophia Grace'. YouTube, 16 January. https://www.youtube.com/watch?v=7A6V5uW92CY

@SophiaGrace (2016c). 'Sophia Grace | Morning routine'. YouTube, 10 May. https://www.youtube.com/watch?v=EOPbL9cWzMw

@SophiaGrace (2016d). 'Sophia Grace | In New York'. YouTube, 26 June. https://www.youtube.com/watch?v=rxVIO95N-1M

@SophiaGrace (2016e). 'Sophia Grace Q&A'. YouTube, 7 July. https://www.youtube.com/watch?v=TIwUnMcok4k

@SophiaGrace (2016f). 'Sophia Grace – Flying with my sister "Belle"'. YouTube, 14 December. https://www.youtube.com/watch?v=3Lgkdu93ikc

@SophiaGrace (2017a). 'Making Slime | Sophia Grace & Rebecca Zamalo – Testing Instagram slime'. YouTube, 27 July. https://www.youtube.com/watch?v=1s181OMzdu0

@SophiaGrace (2017b). 'Oreo challenge | Sophia Grace & Jessii Vee – blindfold taste test!!!' YouTube, 17 August. https://www.youtube.com/watch?v=yCXXUWLbR8c

@SophiaGrace (2017c). 'Who is my boyfriend?! Sophia Grace Q&A'. YouTube, 31 March. https://www.youtube.com/watch?v=niu3CCWhzpw

@SophiaGrace (2017d). 'Sophia Grace | Makeup tutorial 2017'. YouTube, 8 June. https://www.youtube.com/watch?v=-e9u22Z5kdQ

@SophiaGrace (2022). 'Im pregnant. . . | Sophia Grace'. YouTube, 23 October. https://www.youtube.com/watch?v=ysPlVnAJ3_Y

@TEAMTITANOFFICIAL (2019). 'JianHao and Debbie's baby is here! – Team Titan Vlogs'. YouTube, 22 September. https://www.youtube.com/watch?v=XVqRRhdup_Q

@TEAMTITANOFFICIAL (2024). 'Team Titan Official'. YouTube. https://www.youtube.com/@TEAMTITANOFFICIAL/videos

@TheEllenShow (2011a). 'Sophia Grace's show stopping performance!' YouTube, 12 October. https://www.youtube.com/watch?v=odhUPMYXpX4

@TheEllenShow (2011b). 'Nicki Minaj sings "Super Bass" with Sophia Grace (Full Version)'. YouTube, 12 October. https://www.youtube.com/watch?v=f9573kGBtuE

@TheEllenShow (2011c). 'Sophia and Rosie dance during break'. YouTube, 12 October. https://www.youtube.com/watch?v=RALcbuWaWE0

@TheEllenShow (2011d). 'Sophia Grace and Rosie: AMA correspondents!' YouTube, 7 November. https://www.youtube.com/watch?v=JJB-Wx7l8A0

@TheEllenShow (2011e). 'Sophia Grace and Rosie hit the red carpet!' YouTube, 22 November. https://www.youtube.com/watch?v=KUWpd91UBrA

@TheEllenShow (2012a). 'Exclusive: Sophia Grace & Rosie bonus VMA footage'. YouTube, 11 September. https://www.youtube.com/watch?v=zvoXMFNIcbg

@TheEllenShow (2012b). 'Sophia Grace & Rosie love target'. YouTube, 10 May. https://www.youtube.com/watch?v=ar97Iu-5qh4

@TheEllenShow (2012c). 'Sophia Grace & Rosie meet Fijit!' YouTube, 2 October. https://www.youtube.com/watch?v=0-MsShNsKgY

@TheEllenShow (2012d). 'Sophia Grace & Rosie have 100M views on YouTube!' YouTube, 25 April. https://www.youtube.com/watch?v=Aspr2r9km3Y

@TheEllenShow (2012e). 'Sophia Grace & Rosie on America'. YouTube, 2 May. https://www.youtube.com/watch?v=HZFkB4lS_7Q

@TheEllenShow (2012f). 'Web exclusive: Sophia Grace and Rosie backstage!' YouTube, 20 February. https://www.youtube.com/watch?v=UVwJMCK8I40

@TheEllenShow (2012g). 'Backstage with Sophia Grace and Rosie'. YouTube, 14 March. https://www.youtube.com/watch?v=faEz5L62pTA

@TheEllenShow (2012h). 'Exclusive! Rainer and Atticus meet Sophia Grace & Rosie'. YouTube, 19 September. https://www.youtube.com/watch?v=C8neQ4T-cHQ

@TheEllenShow (2013a). 'Exclusive! Sophia Grace & Rosie bonus Grammy footage!' YouTube, 11 February. https://www.youtube.com/watch?v=BpPpEJenhV8

@TheEllenShow (2013b). 'Exclusive! Sophia Grace & Rosie meet the Disney princesses'. YouTube, 16 May. https://www.youtube.com/watch?v=FzVk9-9XAow

@TheEllenShow (2013c). '"Tea Time" with Sophia Grace & Rosie'. YouTube, 31 May. https://www.youtube.com/watch?v=AUIep_UoKUc&list=PLuW4g7xujBWcaDNqBoQqlbXqBzXE5nyNA

@TheEllenShow (2013d). 'Sophia Grace & Rosie on their new book and movie!' YouTube, 15 November. https://www.youtube.com/watch?v=zns6hZu6FRQ

@TheEllenShow (2013e). 'Sophia Grace & Rosie on their dream jobs'. YouTube, 6 May. https://www.youtube.com/watch?v=rZHFkDzOxEs

@TheEllenShow (2013f). 'Sophia Grace & Rosie on becoming big sisters!' YouTube, 8 November. https://www.youtube.com/watch?v=Zpb2ChlEfi8

@TheEllenShow (2013g). 'Sophia Grace & Rosie are back!' YouTube, 4 November. https://www.youtube.com/watch?v=W3Y7stDfvH0

@TheEllenShow (2014a). 'World premiere! Sophia Grace & Rosie's movie!' YouTube, 17 March. https://www.youtube.com/watch?v=ZP8ZnAIwdA4

@TheEllenShow (2014b). 'Sophia Grace & Rosie on their new siblings'. YouTube, 15 May. https://www.youtube.com/watch?v=bwbbOL2HTyU

@TheEllenShow (2014c). 'Sophia Grace & Rosie return to Ellen!' YouTube, 2 April. https://www.youtube.com/watch?v=2Fq_1IUwHf4

@TheEllenShow (2015). 'The return of Sophia Grace & Rosie'. YouTube, 19 November. https://www.youtube.com/watch?v=XcorLEso5J8

@TheEllenShow (n.d.). 'Adorable kids [YouTube playlist]'. YouTube. [Link since removed]

@therealsophiagrace (2023). '26.02.23♡'. Instagram, 5 March. https://www.instagram.com/p/CpbBtbgK6Ie/

@Xiaxue (2018). 'Vlog with Dash – Fun activities to do with your toddler at home!' YouTube, 5 March. www.youtube.com/watch?v=9RmYRD05Vfk

Index

Note: *Italic* page numbers refer to *figures* and **Bold** page numbers reference to **tables**.